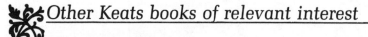 # Other Keats books of relevant interest

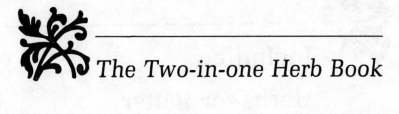

The Two-in-one Herb Book

Including

Herbs for Better Body Beauty
by Alyson Huxley
&
Herbs for Cooking, Cleaning, Canning and Sundry Household Chores
by Philippa Back

The Two-in-one Herb Book

Illustrated by
Linda Diggins

Keats Publishing, Inc. New Canaan, Connecticut

THE TWO-IN-ONE-HERB BOOK

Keats edition published 1982

Incorporating *Herbs for Better Body Beauty* by Alyson Huxley originally published as *Natural Beauty with Herbs*

Herbs for Cooking, Cleaning, Canning and Sundry Household Chores by Philippa Back, originally published as *Herbs about the House*

Published by arrangement with Darton, Longman and Todd, Ltd., London
Special contents copyright © 1982 by Keats Publishing, Inc.

Library of Congress Catalog Card Number: 81-82166
ISBN: 0-87983-225-8

Printed in the United States of America

Keats Publishing, Inc., 36 Grove Street (Box 876)
New Canaan, Connecticut   06840

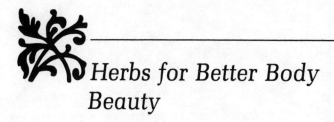

Herbs for Better Body Beauty

Contents
Herbs for Better
Body Beauty

An appendix, providing a list of suppliers will be
found at the end of The Two-in-One Herb Book.

 Introduction

Unless you are in perfect good health your skin and hair will look dull and lifeless, and unless you are scrupulously clean, any creams or lotions, however exclusive or expensive, will just not have a fair chance to work to their best advantage.

In helping us to be totally clean and to make the best of what looks we have, hundreds of cleansing and cosmetic items have been created through the ages, but never before has there been such a vast array, or such clever advertising to persuade us to buy a particular range of goods—each one trying to outdo the other in their claims of super-efficiency at their task, each company putting forward "new" gimmicks in an attempt at increasing sales. The cosmetics market is swamped with goods to aid us in our pursuit of good looks.

Beauty, as we know is a natural attribute and its enhancement should, I feel, as far as possible, be derived from products made of natural ingredients. By natural, I mean non-animal ingredients—except lanolin, which comes from sheep's wool, beeswax and honey, none of which entail cruelty in their collection.

Many ingredients in cosmetics are of animal origin; for example cleansing and moisturizing creams often contain emulsifying waxes or stearic acids, which may derive in part or whole from whale oil or tallow, which is animal fat; cuticle creams contain petroleum jelly, obtained from an extract of petroleum and filtered through animal charcoal; shampoos and soaps are often made from tallow, turtle or mink oils. Perfumes may contain musk from the musk deer, rat or ox, castoreum from beavers, ambergris from whales or civet from the civet cat.

These ingredients are sometimes obtained in extremely cruel ways. Not only the collection of the ingredients but also the ways in which they are tested in laboratories involve suffering; helpless little animals such as guinea-pigs, mice and rabbits endure irritation and pain in the course of man's finding out the effects of shampoos, coloring agents and other cosmetic items—and even the effects of preservative additions to creams and lotions.

A nasty picture by any standards and in fact not at all necessary since harmless non-animal alternatives are available. These alternatives are in fact what this book is about.

Throughout history people have experimented on themselves with all kinds of ingredients for cosmetic use in their pursuit of beauty; with plants and other good things like honey or eggs. I have tracked down many of these recipes and recorded them, in modern terms as far as possible, for use today.

ONE

Herbal cosmetics in history

It is probable, though by no means certain, that the use of cosmetics originated in China over 4,000 years ago. A lot of general information on herbs and their uses was gathered together and recorded in the first "herbal" by the Chinese emperor Shen Nung, in 3000 B.C. The book dealt with the medicinal and culinary use of plants; cosmetics presumably being considered too frivolous for inclusion in such a serious work.

Though ancient Sumerian and Egyptian records also exist, it is generally thought that their chief source of information was from China.

The earliest evidence of cosmetics comes from Egypt, where, along with the mummified bodies of pharaohs and their consorts, it was customary to bury examples of the comforts and luxuries available to them in their earthly lifetime for use in their afterlife. The cosmetics included kohl, made from antimony, for painting the eyebrows and around the eyes, various eye "shadows" of mineral origin, and henna powder which was used not only as a hair dye but also for coloring the finger and toenails as well as the palms of the hands and soles of the feet. There is also evidence that mud from the river Nile was used as the basis of a face mask.

Perfumes were mostly sesame oil-based or wine-based,

as the art of perfume distillation had not been discovered. Kyphi, the name of a once sacred Egyptian perfume, originally used for embalming, was made from myrrh, cyprinum, cinnamon, juniper, honey and raisins steeped in wine. Many other fragrant oils were used, chiefly as body rubs, skin softeners and as additions to bathing water. These were prepared from a variety of ingredients, some specially imported, such as frankincense, spikenard, iris root, sandal and cedar wood, as well as locally produced aromatic herbs.

Throughout the ancient world the Egyptians were renowned for their skills in cosmetics and through their trade in perfumes much of their knowledge was passed on to other cultures.

The Mesopotamians, like the Egyptians, were very particular about personal cleanliness and used many plant "juices," such as tamarisk, pine and date palm, for cleansing the skin.

Greek women used few cosmetics, except for the courtesans, who lavishly decorated themselves as an advertisement for their trade. The ordinary wife was considered a child-bearer and home manager and not an object of pleasure and beauty, so her use of cosmetics was limited to the subtle coloring of lips and cheeks with a vegetable dye probably derived from alkanet or bugloss. The only exception in the use of cosmetics was where hair was concerned, and its color would be changed at whim, using various powdered minerals, dried plants or their juices.

In the first century A.D., Dioscorides compiled a massive book on herbs and their uses, which was to become a standard source of information for hundreds of years. Presumably many of the plants mentioned as being suitable for providing dyes for cloth were also experimented with on human hair.

Galen, a Greek physician who lived in the second century A.D., discovered that vegetable oil could be mixed with water and melted beeswax, and that the resulting cream, when smoothed on the skin, was cool and soothing; not only did the skin become soft but it also became supple. He had, though he did not know it, discovered what we know today as "cold cream."

The Romans in their turn learned their cosmetic skills from the Egyptians; unlike the Greeks all Romans used them. Hair dyes were also very popular, many recipes having come from Gaul and Germany. Bleaches for hair were often made from soap compounds, but as Roman hair was less strong than that of their conquered people they often lost a lot of it, or their once glowing dark tresses became coarse and brassy. Gray hair did not respond to this soap-bleach so it was advised that the hairs be restored to their original color by using the green outsides of walnuts. This worked quite well, but the juice had to be used as freshly as possible for best effect.

The generally poor condition of hair then led to the creation of "conditioning cream," which attempted to restore the original lustre and texture: one recipe contained pepper and hellebore mixed with rats' heads and droppings! On the whole the restoring efforts had little good effect, so what little hair was left had to be hidden under a wig—usually made from the golden locks of captive Germans.

Unwanted bodily hair could be removed by covering it with a mixture of yellow arsenic sulphide known as orpiment, and lime, or by rubbing it with pumice.

According to Ovid, a Roman lady upon going to bed would cover her face with a mask made of barley flour, bean flour, eggs, powdered narcissus bulbs and honey (rather sticky to sleep in), and Juvenal mentions the use of "the sweat of sheep's wool" as a night cream—it sounds awful but is in fact lanolin. The day started with washing off the sticky face mask with scented water and cleaning teeth with powdered pumice mixed with vinegar. A revolting habit, introduced from Spain, was of rubbing the teeth with stale urine.

Bathing, though originally an Egyptian idea, was only to reach its peak in Roman times. Public bath houses were common enough, but to have a private bath in one's house was considered to be the height of luxury.

Bathing was a leisurely affair, the water being hot and sweetly scented with lavender from Germany, rosewater from Phaselis or marjoram from Cos. Poppaea, Nero's wife, even kept a large herd of wild asses, just so that she would always be able to bathe in milk.

Soap for cleansing the skin was not used until A.D. 160

and then only for medical rather than pleasurable reasons. A mixture of olive oil and pumice was rubbed on to the body and then removed with a long narrow scraper called a "strigil." After a bath came a massage with fragrant oils and creams.

When clean and sweet-smelling a lady would paint her face "fashionably white" with powdered white lead mixed with chalk, line her eyes with kohl, tint her cheeks and lips with red ochre or "Syrian root," and shape her eyebrows by plucking. Finally her slave would arrange and adorn her hair, whether her own or a wig, and help her to dress.

While the Romans were ruining their hair and complexions, Indian women were mastering the arts of cosmetic adornment and allurement. Bathing and making-up had deep religious significance and to be physically alluring was of great importance. Water was perfumed with patchouli, jasmine or sandalwood. After washing, many different pale colored and scented oils were rubbed on to various parts of the body to lighten the color of the skin. Eyes were lined with kohl made from lampblack mixed with oil, lips stained vermilion and the soles of the feet stained with henna, as were the arms and hands, the latter in intricately painted designs.

The Chinese, like the Romans, used cosmetics liberally. Anyone who had any regard for the condition of their complexion covered their faces at night with a mask of tea oil and rice flour, which they carefully scraped off the following morning. Next they spread on a white powder, known as "Meen-Fun," and painted their lips, cheeks and nostrils with carmine, the color of which was then toned down with a dusting of loose rice powder. The pulp from a fruit called "Lung-ju-en" was sometimes used as a base for a special kind of cold cream and teeth were cleaned with a powder made from finely ground sea shells.

Cosmetics were first used in Britain at the time of the Roman occupation. The conquered peoples had previously only known creams and potions as medicines with magical powers, to be applied while special words were recited, rather than something to be used for purely aesthetic and pleasurable reasons. A civilized and sophisticated way of life was, after some years, adopted by the Celts, but gradually, after the

Romans left, the many invasions from barbaric tribes led to the decline of the civilized life the people had come to accept and enjoy. These wild tribes re-introduced body painting with woad and tattooing, so the finer points of Roman life were slowly forgotten.

As Christianity spread, the idea of personal adornment and bathing were frowned upon as vain and heathen and a reminder of the corruption and wickedness that led to the fall of Rome. In spite of the loss of cosmetics and perfumes there was a revival in the use of herbal potions and lotions concocted by local witches.

As far as the enhancement of beauty was concerned the Anglo-Saxons and the Normans remained somewhat ignorant until the time of the Crusades, when homeward bound knights brought back the knowledge of many of the customs and commodities which they had appreciated while in the Middle East.

Bathing was again to become a popular pastime, using water that contained a variety of fragrant herbs. The onetime witches, too, made cosmetics which they sold along with their love potions and medicinal ointments.

Blonde and black hair became fashionable—red being associated with witches and the devil. Herbal skin lotions and creams, previously used as treatment for rashes, became used generally as face and body creams. Preparations for soothing sore eyes and rough skin and for lightening hair were made from recipes including aloes, laurel berries, pepper, lily of the valley, foxgloves and mint.

Superfluous hair was again removed with pumice or special cream: at one time it was the height of fashion to completely pluck away the eyebrows, leaving a large expanse of white forehead. A white skin was essential for those who wished to be considered the least bit attractive, the merest hint of a tan or freckles had to be hidden behind a mask of powdered wheat.

English women were so intimidated by the Church and its teachings, which condemned vanity as an evil, that it took some time before cosmetics were used openly and unashamedly. Women of the French Court, it would seem, were less afraid and used what they wanted, and were in fact to be influential in English fashions as well. The general acceptance of cosmetics did not begin until the end of the fifteenth century.

In 1526 in England, Peter Treveris produced and printed what was to become known as *The Grete Herbal*. It was a translation of a French work based on a manuscript written centuries earlier, which contained many recipes for "hygienic" cosmetics, which could be prepared from plant ingredients. Examples were a complexion water made from borax and rosewater; cuttlefish bone powder for polishing teeth; water collected from the bark of the willow tree, for clearing blemishes and dandruff, and cucumber and cowslip juice for removing freckles. For their "aesthetic" cosmetic recipes English women had to look to France where in 1530 a physician called André le Fournier produced a book full of useful ideas.

Elizabeth I was one of the first to adopt the use of the cosmetics that came from France and it was she, with her naturally pale skin and light red hair, who was to set the standards for the fashionable Tudor beauty.

Faces were whitened with ceruse (white lead), or a mixture of sulfur and borax powdered with finely ground alabaster or perfumed starch and "set" with a film of eggwhite, cheeks rouged with ochre or mercuric sulphide, and lips colored with a salve made of cochineal mixed with gum arabic, fig "milk" and eggwhite. Eyes were made to sparkle and appear girlishly wide and innocent with drops of bella-donna (nightshade), and were lined with kohl. Hair had to be either red or golden; red was achieved by washing in "honey residew" or henna, and golden with turmeric, rhubarb steeped in wine or by a rinse of saffron water. Eyebrows were again plucked away—a return to the medieval habit—so too was the hairline to give greater length to the face. It was also a fashionable compliment for men to dye their beards the color of the Queen's hair, with a dye made from radishes and hedge-privet.

Elizabeth I is attributed with inventing and using several cosmetics and perfumes; one lotion contained eggs and their shells, burnt alum, sugar, borax and poppy seeds mixed with water.

Mary Queen of Scots, Elizabeth's cousin, is reputed to have bathed in wine and to have had a fine white skin as a result.

In France, Henry III used nightly face masks of flour and eggwhite, washed off with chervil water, and it was he who started the fashion for men to use skin lotions and perfumes.

The soaps of the time were still coarse and unsuitable for cleaning the skin; any washing—and precious little of it there seems to have been—had to be done with floral waters. Even the Queen only resorted to a bath once a month, and then no doubt she used a "washing-ball" containing a little flaked soap and lots of herbs. The general lack of interest in personal cleanliness gave rise to the lavish use of perfumes of all kinds, not only in liquid form, but also used on gloves, in pot-pourris, pomanders, and in hundreds of different ways of scenting the hair and clothes.

In 1602 Sir Hugh Platt produced one of the first household recipe books, called *Delightes for Ladies*, which included all sorts of recipes for cosmetics: how to bleach the skin with lemon juice and bitter almonds or rosemary boiled in wine; how to fade freckles with either birch sap or elderflower water; how to clear a blemished skin with turpentine or resins, and instructions for cleaning the teeth with a dentifrice made from gum tragacanth and ground alabaster.

A few years later, Gervase Markham in one of his works recommends the use of a herbal milk bath made from rosemary, fennel, violets and nettles boiled in milk, and William Vaughn in his book of *Naturall and Artificial Directions for Health*, published in 1600, advised washing the hair in woodash and water.

When Charles I came to the throne, the English Court was very much influenced by the taste of his French wife Henrietta Maria. Fashions changed considerably but cosmetics were still similar to those used in Elizabeth's time; with the additional use of such luxuries as French orange flower water and apricot paste, new perfumes from Italy and gentle castile soap from Spain.

Though John Gerard first published his famous herbal in

1597, it was not until the appearance of the 1633 revised edition that it gained in popularity. The recipes were mainly medicinal but many of them were used effectively for general good health and to condition both skin and hair. One face lotion contained orrisroot, camphire, blanched almonds, oak apples and lemon juice; this being recommended not only for clearing the complexion but also for soothing sunburn. And in 1652 Nicholas Culpeper published a book of herbal medicines and natural cosmetics based on the works of Hippocrates and Pliny. Many of his recipes have been used effectively ever since and are still popular today. It was he who suggested rinsing hair in an infusion of chamomile, and using parsley for soothing sore eyes, among a host of other ideas.

Charles II in his "friendship" with Nell Gwynn, was inadvertently to popularize the use of make-up to a theatrical extreme. Skin was still whitened with ceruse, but it was mixed with water or eggwhite and applied with a damp cloth; less harmful than the old, pure, white lead used by the Elizabethans. Pock marks and other facial blemishes were hidden under "patches" of varying size and shape.

Another book, containing much advice on cleanliness and the making of cosmetics, was written by Thomas Jeamson in 1665. All imaginable kinds of ingredients were mixed together to form pastes and pomades: cucumber, bryony, daffodil, date pits, lupins and coral, to name but a few items in one recipe for a freckle eliminator. One thing he was most concerned about was unpleasant perspiration odor and its removal; he suggested bathing underarms with alum dissolved in water, or a more elaborate lotion containing bryony roots, friars cowl, pellitory of the wall, elecampagne, beans, rice, vetch, barley and chamomile. Quite a harvest festival in itself!

In 1684 a herbalist named George Wilson was appointed by James II to make special "Honey Water" face lotion for him, which contained honey, lemon rind, cloves, nutmeg, gum storax and gum bezoin, coriander and vanilla.

1709 saw the invention of what later became known as Eau de Cologne; it was a blend of pure alcohol, bergamot, lemon oil, rosemary and orange, and has changed very little to this day. Two other popular eaux de toilette were lavender water and "Hungary Water," made from rosemary, peppermint, orange and lemon, rosewater and alcohol—a recipe said to have been given to Queen Elizabeth of Hungary in 1235 by a hermit.

Both men and women of this time wore most elaborate make-up; it was a time of supremely artificial beauty when thick white-lead masks were needed to hide the ravages of smallpox. People with unblemished skins also wore these masks purely to follow fashion. Their one-time good complexions must have deteriorated at quite a rate, all the facial pores being constantly clogged with layers of powdered white lead. In fact many notable beauties died from lead poisoning.

In 1724 an Act was passed through Parliament, to ensure very careful examination of ingredients in cosmetics and though, as a result, many did become less harmful and safer to use, old habits died hard and a lot of people still preferred the old lead-based cosmetics.

Towards the end of the eighteenth century, possibly as a result of this Act, there was a slight swing to the use of safe cosmetics and many suggested recipes were put forward in an English version of the originally French *Toilet of Flora*.

With the French revolution came the end of aristocratic society and of the extravagant use of cosmetics. The revolution also saw the end of the strong French influence on society in London.

Throughout most of the nineteenth century, brightly colored cosmetics were anathema. The fashion was for ladies to look naturally delicate and pretty and men to look masculine. Cosmetics were made from flowers, herbs and vegetable oils, pure, natural and safe ingredients as compared with previously evil eighteenth-century concoctions.

The importance of natural ingredients led to many books being written on the subject, encouraging housewives to make their own cosmetics at home; preparations aiming to improve the natural condition of skin and hair instead of artificially concealing it. Cleanliness too was encouraged: unpleasant body odors could no longer be camouflaged by the new gentler fragranced perfumes, so a clean body was essential. It was advised to scrub the body vigorously in hot water or to have steam baths followed by the application of fragrant herbal lotions and ointments.

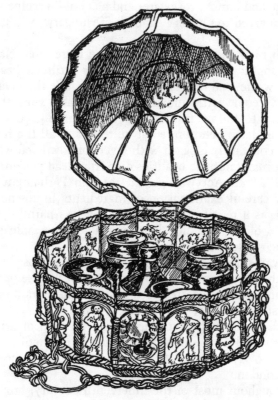

*An old
cosmetic box*

Fashion still dictated the importance of white skin and so there were numerous recipes for lightening it and removing freckles, containing nothing stronger than milk, horseradish juice or lemon. Cheeks were very subtly rouged with sandalwood or saffron mixed with talcum powder.

In spite of the new-found art in the use of make-up, during Queen Victoria's reign it was considered highly unfashionable, even immoral, to use cosmetics. A daily bath was considered essential among those who had the facilities for it—"cleanliness was next to Godliness"—and so led to the increased manufacture and improvement of soaps and the reduction of its previously scandalous price (because of taxation).

Any female attempts at self-improvement were frowned

upon—anything used had to be done in secret and with such subtlety that it was hardly noticeable.

Vanity in women was, as in the days of early Christianity in Europe, considered evil. Young girls were warned that the use of cosmetics would give the men the impression that they were promiscuous. On the other hand men used whatever hair dyes and lotions they pleased with no questions asked.

With the start of the National Society for Women's Suffrage, in 1868, women began to come out of their shells and not only voiced their opinions on previously tabooed subjects but also did what they saw fit to do. A new image of feminine beauty emerged, highlighted by actresses such as Sarah Bernhardt, Ellen Terry and Lily Langtry, who adopted the use of cosmetics off stage as well as on—carmine lip color, eyes enhanced with kohl and powder shadows, and lashes with mascara of coconut oil and lampblack.

The habit of making cosmetics at home was to lose popularity in favor of shop-bought items and as a result several cosmetic houses were founded, which, through clever advertisements, encouraged women to buy their goods.

The advent and increasing popularity of the movies brought about a marked increase in the use of cosmetics. Not only did Society use them, everyone now did, and tried to copy the faces of their favorite film stars. Mascara was now made from fine soot or burnt senna mixed with soap, and lipstick from alkanet root or carmine (made from cochineal) mixed with beeswax and lanolin. With the mass use of cosmetics and the increasing number of cosmetic houses, it became necessary for gimmicks to boost sales of particular items and even whole ranges of preparations.

With the emancipation of women came too a desire for a more open and active way of life, and among other things more vigorous outdoor sports were taken up. Gradually it became fashionable to sport a naturally lightly suntanned and healthy skin: at last the pale beauty was beginning to lose popularity. With this preference for darker skin came the need for colored face creams and powders and darker shades of lipstick and nail polish; the whiter-than-white face masks and powders were put aside.

During the first half of the Second World War girls joining the British forces were given lists of cosmetic substitutes, such as potato juice, lemon juice and eggs—and their possible uses—but in time these items proved more difficult to obtain than the cosmetics they were trying to replace. The importance of cosmetics as a boost to morale was realized, so much so that both lipstick and powder became standard issue.

In post-war years the cosmetic trade gained new impetus: the ranges of goods available with their now reasonable prices, increased to such an extent that no one gave a thought to actually making their own at home.

Since the 1960s the range of cosmetics as well as clothing fashions have been limitless. Haute Couture may provide a "look" each season which a minority copy to the letter, but in general people tend to "do their own thing" and wear just what pleases them.

One trend in make-up which has been popular for some years now is that of using goods which contain only pure and natural ingredients; this in turn has led to a revival and an increasing interest in the art of home-made cosmetics, but it must not be believed that everything that comes out of a factory is automatically bad nor that everything from natural sources is good. For instance, suffering is caused to whales, musk deer and civet cats, to name a few, in the collection of oils, waxes and musk grains for the cosmetic and perfumery industries—all perfectly natural ingredients it is true, but why should such unnecessary pain be caused when there are perfectly acceptable non-animal alternatives available?

A few cosmetic manufacturers have made the effort to avoid these animal ingredients. In England a charitable trust called Beauty Without Cruelty was founded in 1959, with the aim of publicizing the facts of the cruelty caused to animals in the pursuit of beauty, and to find alternatives to animal ingredients; many high quality cosmetics are now produced, created from oils and essences from herbs and flowers, which in fact have been proven to be far superior to similar goods containing ingredients of animal origin.

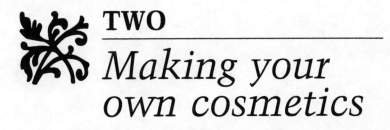

TWO

Making your own cosmetics

Assuming you have the time and the wish to make your own cosmetics it can not only prove to be money saving but also great fun and very rewarding.

It may be simple enough to go to a shop to buy whatever you need, but first think how much more satisfying it would be to actually use your own exclusive brand—possibly containing herbs you've grown yourself too—and to know exactly what each item contains. You will feel happy knowing that you at least are not increasing the demand for goods which might in some way have caused pain to a helpless animal, in your pursuit of beauty.

Once you have learned to make cosmetics why not encourage your friends to do the same—give them samples of yours to persuade them. Try to spread the knowledge of beauty and its enhancement without the need for cruelty.

The recipes given are basically for "hygienic" cosmetics rather than "aesthetic" ones—which means that they are also suitable for men—after all they too wash their hair, take baths and have need of dusting powders, deodorants, skin lotions and creams.

I am not giving you strict instructions to be followed to the letter, just an idea of what you could do. All the recipes are flexible and quantities and ingredients can be varied as you get familiar with the processes and their results—but don't expect your finished products to look exactly like shop-bought ones because they won't: you haven't the facilities nor the super-fine equipment.

All herbs used are dried unless stated otherwise. Dried herbs have about twice the strength of fresh ones, so if you particularly want to use fresh where I state dried simply double the quantity to achieve a similar result.

The quantities of ingredients in recipes are purposely small as there is no point in making a vast quantity of one thing only to find that you don't really like it or that it doesn't suit your skin. For instance, I know someone who, although she can eat honey, gets a nasty rash if it is applied to her skin in any guise. On the whole the recipes are not perfumed with added scenting oils, as it is sometimes this ingredient to which people are allergic. If you think your skin will be safe, add a few drops of whatever essential oils you like until the smell pleases you. The best way is to make a little—try it—and if it suits you make a bigger batch.

When you've settled for a particular item don't make absolutely masses, hoping to save time and money, because these goodies do not contain preservatives. Make a sensible amount and store it in the refrigerator, but only for a month or so, and do be sure that all tops and lids fit snugly.

Note the section "An ABC of Herbal Terms," a glossary of processes, ingredients, etc.

Making cosmetics at home does not involve great chemical knowledge or extra-special equipment. Basically you will need:

an enamel double boiler or a Pyrex bowl that will fit neatly into a saucepan (for melting oils and waxes over slow heat)

a small wooden spoon

another Pyrex bowl

a fine sieve or pieces of muslin or cheesecloth

a fork

a whisk or an electric blender and beater (invaluable but not essential) pestle and mortar (a bowl and spoon will do)

a palette knife or other knife with flexible blade

1 tablespoon, 1 teaspoon

a measuring cup

an eyedropper

a plastic bowl-scraper (for getting every scrap of cream into its jar)

rubber gloves

and:

a good supply of small screw-top plastic or glass jars, tubs and bottles

self-adhesive labels (for labelling everything as soon as you make it; later on you're bound to forget)

A word of warning: never use aluminum or non-stick pans or utensils when making cosmetics—it could be dangerous.

Before you start making your cosmetics, do you know what type of skin and hair you have? Nobody's is ever of just one type so you will need different lotions and creams for specific areas and problems.

DRY

Skin is tightly drawn over bones and is often flaky. Use rich cleansing creams followed by toning herbal infusions, and moisturize with rich nourishing creams. Improve condition with oils. Use a good moisturizing face mask once a week, followed by a rich nourishing cream.

NORMAL

Skin feels smooth, is finely textured and soft. Cleanse with lotions or light creams or milk. Tone with a mild freshener such as rosewater and use a light moisturizer; have a weekly face mask followed by a light moisturizer.

OILY

Often shiny and prone to blackheads or spots. May need cleansing several times a day with soap or lotion followed by an astringent. Use a drying mask once a week and wash with a mild astringent lotion afterwards.

SENSITIVE

Usually finely textured but sometimes with reddish patches, often reacts violently to perfumed cosmetics. Cleanse with a light cream or milk and tone with a herbal infusion. Moisturize dry areas only. Use a mild face mask occasionally, followed by a light moisturizer.

Start your top to toe natural beauty campaign now by deciding what you need and where you need it most and make and use your own accordingly.

For the hair

SHAMPOOS

Mild and gentle shampoo

½ oz. or approximately 6 tablespoons crushed soapwort root
5 cups boiling water

Put the soapwort in a bowl and cover with boiling water. Leave it to steep for 15 minutes, then strain and use half a cup of the liquid to shampoo your hair.

Mild herbal shampoo

6 tablespoons crushed soapwort root
6 tablespoons chamomile flowers or rosemary leaves or horsetail
5 cups boiling water

Put the soapwort and the herbs in a bowl and pour over the boiling water. Leave it to steep for 15 minutes, strain and wash hair with a cupful of the liquid.

Floral shampoo
1 tablespoon of flowers or herbs
1½ tablespoons borax
1½ tablespoons sodium sesquicarbonate
2 tablespoons flaked soap

Carefully combine the ingredients with a pestle and mortar. To use, dissolve 2 tablespoons of the powder in ¼ cup of hot water and leave to steep for a few minutes until cool enough to use.

Lemon shampoo
2 cups boiling water
1 cup lemon balm leaves
2 tablespoons sodium sesquicarbonate
5 tablespoons of flaked soap
a few drops of oil of lemon

With 1 cup boiling water make an infusion of the lemon balm: in the other cup melt the sodium sesquicarbonate and the flaked soap. Strain the infusion and combine both liquids, adding the oil of lemons. Use about a cupful to shampoo your hair.

Egg and orange shampoo
1 egg yolk
1 tablespoon orange juice
1 cup of soapwort infusion

Beat the egg yolk and the orange juice into the soapwort infusion and shampoo your hair using warm water.

If you have particularly greasy hair, cleaning it with a "dry" shampoo may be helpful in reducing excess oils; or perhaps your hair could do with a wash but you haven't time for a "wet" shampoo. Either way try one of these dry shampoos for a quick clean.

Dry "root" shampoo
1 tablespoon arrowroot powder
1 tablespoon orrisroot powder

Mix the powders together and sprinkle into your hair, work it well into the scalp and all over your head. Leave on for 10 minutes and then brush out every trace of powder with a fine bristled brush.

Rosemary dry shampoo
few drops oil of rosemary
1 tablespoon fuller's earth powder

Add the oil to the powder and blend it carefully in a pestle and mortar. When the oil has been absorbed by the powder sift it and sprinkle the powder into your hair as with the dry "root" shampoo.

An even quicker shampoo for real emergencies is to dab some lavender water or rosewater on your hair—rub in and briskly brush your hair with it. Repeat this until any trace of greasiness has gone and your hair is sweet smelling.

CONDITIONERS

If you have dry or brittle hair, any of the vegetable oils can act as a marvellous conditioner.

Oil conditioner
2 tablespoons vegetable oil

Slowly heat the oil in a double boiler. When warmed massage it into your scalp and all through your hair; then cover the

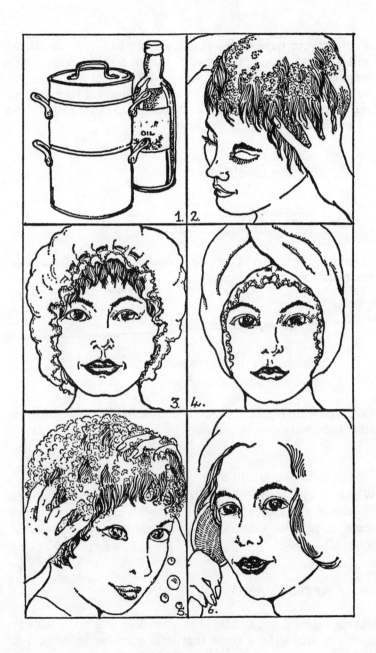

Using an oil conditioner

whole of your head with a plastic shower hat (a polythene bag will do just as well). Cover that, turban fashion, with a well warmed towel (the quickest way is to soak it in hot water and wring out the surplus). When the towel goes cold repeat once and then shampoo your hair as usual making sure you remove all excess oil.

Rich hair conditioner
1 egg
1 teaspoon honey
2 teaspoons vegetable oil

Combine these ingredients in a double boiler and massage, steam and shampoo as before.

Egg and apple conditioner
1 egg
1 tablespoon cider vinegar
2 tablespoons vegetable oil

Combine the ingredients in a double boiler and massage, steam and shampoo as before.

Mild hair conditioner
Whisk an egg until fluffy and rub it into your scalp, leave on for about 5 minutes and rinse off with tepid water before shampooing. Don't use hot water or you may get a headful of scrambled egg!

AFTER-SHAMPOO HAIR RINSES

Having cleaned and conditioned your hair you might like to give it a lift with a rinse that will increase shine or add highlights.

Herbal vinegar rinse
½ cup herbal vinegar or cider vinegar
5 cups water

Mix the vinegar with the water and use this solution as a final rinse after shampooing.

HERBAL INFUSION RINSES

Almost any herbs can be infused, singly or mixed, in a final hair-rinsing water—many of them which will leave your hair not only sweet smelling but also very shiny.

Horsetail and sage add shine and enhance color. Parsley and catnip add shine and promote growth. Rosemary and lemon verbena if you have dark hair. Columbine—which smells of hay! Chamomile and yarrow if you have fair hair. Elderflower, southernwood, nettles, lime or quincepeel help prevent dandruff and are generally good for all hair types.

One tablespoon of lemon juice added to the rinsing water is particularly suitable for fair-haired people.

To encourage hair growth mix 2 tablespoons of extract of nasturtium with a few drops of rosemary oil and rub it into the scalp morning and night, brushing your hair thoroughly afterwards, or try rubbing with an infusion of yarrow several times a week.

DANDRUFF TREATMENTS

Should you happen to have dandruff there are some fairly simple ways of getting rid of it.

Nettles and vinegar
Make a strong infusion of nettles and add ½ cup of cider vinegar to it. Massage this into your scalp morning and evening until the dandruff goes.

Rosemary
Add a pinch of borax to an infusion of rosemary leaves and massage into your scalp as before.

HAIR DYES AND COLORANTS

Probably the oldest hair coloring agent is henna. It is almost impossible to predict the exact color change that will take place as the original color and condition of the hair, and the length of time the powder is left on, play such an important part. The only way to get a vague idea is to do a "test" before embarking on what might be an irrevocable step.

Henna powder hair dye
Put some powder in a bowl and to it add enough hot water to make a paste. Wet your hair and with a brush completely cover all your hair or the parts to be colored with the paste. Cover your head with tin foil or a plastic bag and leave until you think your hair is colored sufficiently. Test by cleaning a few strands of hair to see what color change has taken place. The process can be speeded up if you dry the paste with a hair dryer. When completed wash the paste off with warm water and shampoo as usual.
        If you have fair hair you can lighten it quite considerably by making special lightening pastes.

Chamomile hair lightening paste
Make a strong infusion of chamomile flowers and add enough kaolin powder to it to make a paste. Cover all the hair to be lightened with the paste and leave it on for about an hour, then rinse it off with warm water. The first time you use this paste may not be as effective as you thought, but persevere, because successive applications will produce fine results.

Rhubarb hair lightener

Stew two sticks of rhubarb in 1 cup of white wine for about 20 minutes. Leave to steep for a couple of hours and then mix to a paste with kaolin powder. Continue the process as with the previous recipe.

Should you have brown hair that you would like to liven up a bit by adding interesting glints of chestnut, rinse it with a strong infusion of privet leaves. For a slightly lighter shade of chestnut add some quince or apple juice to the infusion.

Walnut brown hair dye

6 *tablespoons green walnut skins*

2 *tablespoons alum powder*

½ *cup orange flower water*

Finely chop up the walnut skins and mix to a paste with the alum and orange flower water. Put the paste onto your hair and leave for about an hour, rinse off with warm water and shampoo as usual.

Gray hair can have a lot of its original color restored if you rinse it with a strong infusion of sage leaves, or mix the infusion to a paste with kaolin powder and proceed as before.

Setting lotions

If you have either limp bodiless hair or straight hair that could do with a bit of bounce, try rinsing it with beer (doesn't matter if it's flat) after a shampoo. It works very well and you won't smell like a brewery either! Lemon juice too works well as a setting lotion, but preferably on light or very greasy hair. Strain the juice of a freshly squeezed lemon and comb it into the hair and set as usual.

A mucilage of quince seeds, made of 2 teaspoons of seeds steeped in ½ cup of hot water makes a firm setting lotion if hair is to be put in curlers. Possibly the simplest method of making a setting lotion is by dissolving 1 table-spoon of sugar in 1 cup of boiling water, and when cool combing that through your hair before setting it.

 For the eyes

To soothe tired eyes:

Make a mild infusion of parsley, chamomile, fennel or colts-foot and, when tepid, use as an eye wash.

Squeeze the juice from ¼ of a cucumber and use that as an eye bath or place 2 slices of it over closed eyes.

Ordinary cold tea can be used to good advantage as an eye lotion, and especially soothing are two tea bags dipped in cold water until the leaves have expanded: squeeze out the excess water and put one over each closed eye, put your feet up and relax for ten minutes.

To reduce puffiness:

Grate a raw potato and put a teaspoonful on two small squares of cotton to cover each closed eye. Put your feet up and leave these compresses on for about 15 minutes and then splash with cold water.

Alternatively, soak two cotton pads in some cooled rose-hip tea, witch hazel or lemon verbena infusion or cucumber juice for soothing eye compresses.

Eye make-up remover

2 tablespoons almond oil
1 tablespoon castor oil

Mix the two oils, soak a piece of cotton in it and gently wipe away any eye make-up.

For teeth, mouth and lips

Tooth cleaning pastes

A very effective but far from attractive paste can be made by crushing some charred bread to a fine powder and mixing it with a few drops of peppermint oil.

Fresh sage leaves crushed with sea salt, baked until hard and re-pounded make a good stain-removing powder.

Fresh sage leaves alone, rubbed over teeth and gums or chewed, are most effective in cleaning, so too are what must be one of the most pleasant of tooth cleaners—fresh strawberries. Rub half a strawberry over your teeth or chew it, or brush them with a fine powder made from pounded dried strawberry roots.

Should you have any doubts as to the freshness and sweetness of your breath try using a decoction of cornflowers or an infusion of mint as a mouth-wash, or even rosewater. Sometimes chewing a couple of cloves or a sprig or two of parsley is effective in purifying the breath.

Breath-fresh pastilles

4 tablespoons lavender flowers
1½ tablespoons icing sugar
enough egg white to bind together

Blend the ingredients together until quite smooth and roll into little balls, leave in a dry place until set firm.

Lip gloss

½ teaspoon beeswax
2 tablespoons cocoa butter

Melt the wax and combine with the cocoa butter. Pour into a pot ready for use. Apply with a lip brush.

For the face

CLEANSING

Many people do not like the idea of cleaning their faces with soap and water—but if done properly it can be of benefit, particularly to anyone with an oily or blemished skin. The best soaps to use as facial cleansers are rich, nourishing ones that will not leave the skin over-dry. Work up a lather using warm water and a soft complexion brush. Spread it all over your face, avoiding the eyes and the delicate skin around them, using a circular movement and paying special attention to the area around your nose. Rinse the lather off with warm water and pat dry with a soft towel, followed by a mild toning lotion or cream. Recipes for soap-making are included in the bathing section.

Oatmeal can be a very effective cleanser both for face and body in general.

Oatmeal cleanser

½ cup oatmeal
4–6 tablespoons milk

Grind the oatmeal to a fine powder, warm the milk and add it to the oatmeal to form a paste. Use this as a facial scrub using a complexion brush as before (a particularly good way of removing dead cells and deep cleansing the pores) and wash off with warm water.

CLEANSING MILKS AND LOTIONS

Yogurt and lemon cleansing milk

1 tablespoon natural yogurt
1 teaspoon lemon juice

Mix the yogurt and the lemon juice and apply to the face with cotton ball or pad. Clean off with tissues.

Herbal buttermilk cleanser
4 tablespoons elderflowers or limeflowers
1 cup buttermilk

Slowly boil the flowers in the buttermilk for about an hour, leave to infuse for at least 2 hours, strain before using.

Mild cleansing milk
¼ cucumber
½ cup of milk

Squeeze the juice from the cucumber and mix it with the milk. Apply to your face with cotton pad and wipe excess off with tissues.

Apple cleansing lotion
1 large apple
1 tablespoon milk
1 tablespoon fuller's earth powder

Squeeze the juice from the apple and combine it with the milk and the powder.

CLEANSING INFUSIONS

Make an average-strength infusion of lemon balm, elderflowers, or limeflowers and use as a cleansing lotion, or use rosewater or orangeflower water.

SIMPLE, NO-EFFORT CLEANSERS

Fresh potato juice or strawberry juice

Warmed milk, natural yogurt

Any of the vegetable oils

CLEANSING CREAMS

Basic light cleansing cream
1 tablespoon beeswax
¼ cup almond oil
¼ teaspoon borax
4 tablespoons distilled water

Slowly melt the wax with the almond oil in a double boiler. Dissolve the borax in the warmed water (do make sure it really has dissolved otherwise your cream will be lumpy). Add the borax solution to the wax and oil. Remove the pan from the heat and stir until cool or beat with a whisk until it thickens and becomes creamy.

Rich avocado cleansing cream
1 oz. or about 2 tablespoons lanolin
1 tablespoon beeswax
¼ cup avocado oil
4 tablespoons distilled water

In a double boiler melt the lanolin and wax and add the oil. When combined, remove the pan from the heat and slowly stir in the water. Stir or whisk until the cream is quite cool.

In both these recipes you can substitute a herbal infusion of your choice instead of the distilled water, or add a few drops of essential oil to add perfume. The vegetable oils too are interchangeable.

Mayonnaise cleansing cream
1 egg
1 tablespoon cider vinegar
½ teaspoon sugar
½ cup olive oil

Cleansing the face—and some of the ingredients you can use

Blend the egg, vinegar and sugar and slowly add the oil, beating all the time, until the mixture thickens and turns golden yellow.

Almond cleansing cream
4 *tablespoons ground almonds*
1 *tablespoon almond oil*
1 *teaspoon quince seeds*
½ *teaspoon borax*
½ *cup hot water*

Dissolve the borax in a little of the hot water. Make a mucilage from the quince seeds and the rest of the hot water and combine the almonds with the almond oil. When the mucilage is ready combine all the ingredients to form a cream.

Irish moss cleansing cream
½ teaspoon borax
½ cup hot water
1 teaspoon Irish moss (carrageen)
4 tablespoons ground almonds
1 tablespoon olive oil

Dissolve the borax in a little of the hot water and use the rest to make a mucilage of the moss. Combine the almonds and the olive oil. When the mucilage is ready, mix all the ingredients together to form a cream.

STEAM CLEANSING

The deepest cleansing treatment is steam, although I do not advise it if your skin is at all sensitive or you have breathing difficulties.

Add a tablespoon of herbs to 2½ cups of boiling water in a large bowl. Hold your face about 12 inches above the bowl and drape a towel over your head and the bowl rim. Steam your face for about 15 minutes. After steaming wipe with cotton pad or tissues to remove impurities and close the pores by splashing with cold water or a herbal infusion. For the total face treatment leave the pores open and apply a face mask followed by a herbal infusion.

Traditionally elderflowers, limeflowers and chamomile flowers have been used as steam facial herbs, but you can experiment with any herbs you like, either singly or combined. Those to be recommended are sage, peppermint, basil, marigold, nasturtium, fennel, thyme, lady's mantle, nettle, yarrow, houseleek and comfrey.

FACE MASKS

Face masks are more effective in cleansing and toning the skin if applied when the pores are open. If you cannot take the steam treatment, try dipping a face cloth into hot water, wringing out the surplus and covering your face with the cloth for a few minutes before applying a mask. Using a mask also can act as a general "pick-me-up" because for it to have a chance to "set" you really need to relax completely with your feet up—normally for about 15 minutes—a good opportunity too for refreshing your eyes with a cool compress.

Almost any herbs, fruits and vegetables can be used in a face mask, either alone, mixed or combined with thickeners such as buttermilk, cream, yogurt, honey, egg, fuller's earth, kaolin powder or oatmeal. Basically what you do is chop a couple of handfuls of herbs and simmer for about 10 minutes in a pan containing either milk or water (enough to prevent them from burning); or mash whatever fruit or vegetables you want to use. If the mixture is particularly runny, thicken it, and cover your face with it leaving eyes and mouth clear. If the idea of actual pieces of vegetation on your face does not appeal, extract the juices and use those instead. Leave the mask on until "set" and wash off with warm water, finally splashing with cold water, a tonic or an astringent lotion to close the pores.

Herbs, fruits, vegetables and other materials for face masks
Parsley

Dandelion, nettle, elderflowers, yarrow, cowslips

Salad burnet, blackberry leaves

Plain egg white beaten until almost stiff

Honey mixed with egg yolk and a teaspoon of oil

Sage mixed with milk and lemon juice

Mashed cucumber mixed with yogurt and kaolin powder

Thick cream mixed with honey

Mashed tomato and oatmeal

Dandelion stewed in milk

Infusion of chamomile mixed with honey and oatmeal

Irish moss or carrageen (mucilage) mixed with oatmeal

Oatmeal and witchhazel

Carrot and yogurt

Avocado mixed with honey and lemon juice

Powdered yeast mixed with yogurt and kaolin powder

Orange juice and honey mixed with buttermilk and oatmeal

Lettuce and yogurt

There are hundreds of variations to the face mask theme so it is just a question of trying anything you like the sound of—or inventing your own.

ASTRINGENT LOTIONS AND SKIN TONICS

Astringent lotions will close the pores of the skin after a face mask, and also help in reducing blackheads and blemishes in general by removing excess oils. Strong lotions usually contain alcohol in some form and should only be used occasionally on particularly greasy skin. The milder lotions and tonics are basically herbal and can be splashed or patted on to the skin more freely and regularly.

Find a small bowl and cut several pieces of cotton or gauze to fit neatly inside it, and soak them in one of the lotions. You will then always have a useful pot of handy freshener pads with which to wipe your face. Any surplus lotion should be wiped off with a tissue. Particularly useful for wiping the face after using a cleansing cream.

STRONG ASTRINGENTS

Rose and witch hazel lotion
¼ *teaspoon borax*
3 *tablespoons herbal infusion*
2 *teaspoons witch hazel*
3 *tablespoons rosewater*

Dissolve the borax in the warmed herbal infusion and when cool combine with the other ingredients.

Herbal vinegar astringent lotion
1 *tablespoon herbal vinegar*
½ *cup distilled water*

Pour into a bottle, shake to combine.

Almond astringent
1 *teaspoon borax*
1½ *teaspoons tincture of benzoin*
1 *cup rosewater*
2 *teaspoons ground almonds*
4 *tablespoons distilled water*

Dissolve the borax in the tincture and add the rosewater to it. Blend the almonds with the distilled water and pour all of it into a bottle. Shake to blend and label it before using.

Simple witch hazel astringent
2 *tablespoons witch hazel*
6 *tablespoons rosewater*

Pour into a bottle, shake and label it.

Camphor lotion
1 teaspoon spirit of camphor
4 tablespoons witch hazel
4 tablespoons orange flower water
4 tablespoons distilled water

Pour into a bottle, shake to combine, and label it.

Marigold lotion
pinch of alum
1 tablespoon witch hazel
6 tablespoons marigold or calendula infusion

Dissolve the alum in the witch hazel and combine with the marigold lotion.

Comfrey astringent
pinch of boric acid
1 tablespoon witch hazel
6 tablespoons comfrey infusion

Dissolve the boric acid in the witch hazel and combine it with the comfrey infusion. Pour into a bottle and leave to stand for a week before using it.

MILD ASTRINGENTS

These are basically herbal infusions which do not contain any spirits.

Parsley, fennel, cowslip, chamomile, yarrow have light astringent properties; they are useful if your skin needs a gentler clean.

Rosemary, nettle, blackberry leaves and dandelion are good generally refreshing, slightly astringent herbs.

Barley boiled in water—strain and use the liquid.

GENERAL SKIN FRESHENER LOTIONS

Rosewater, elderflower water, orangeflower water. Infusion of violets.

For closing large pores, use an infusion of either lady's mantle or horsetail and sage.

Simple skin fresheners—rub a slice of strawberry or cucumber over your face; both these are excellent for a very delicate skin.

WRINKLES, FRECKLES AND AGE-SPOTS

As one gets older the inevitable little wrinkles have a habit of appearing—though these cannot be removed totally they can be softened. Try bathing them with an infusion of chamomile, lemon balm, limeflowers or chervil or cover them with a tightening mask of whisked egg-white. Age can also bring with it those freckle-like brown patches which can be reduced considerably by rubbing them with castor oil or a lotion of watercress juice and honey.

Many people really dislike having a freckled skin; if you are one of them try lightening them by regular use of a decoction of elderflower leaves or tansy, dandelion, lemon juice or one of the following mixtures.

> *1 teaspoon alum*
> *1 tablespoon lemon juice*
> *3 tablespoons elderflower water*
> or
> *1½ teaspoon grated horseradish root stewed in*
> *4 tablespoons of buttermilk, mixed to a paste with*
> *1½ teaspoons of oatmeal*

Only regular application of either paste can make freckles fade, so keep at it and do not sit in the sun either, or they will come back again.

NOURISHING AND MOISTURIZING CREAMS AND LOTIONS

(These are suitable for all parts of the body.)

Rich nourishing cream

2 teaspoons beeswax
1 teaspoon lanolin
4 teaspoons almond oil
pinch of borax
2 tablespoons distilled water
2 capsules wheatgerm oil

Warm the wax, lanolin and almond oil in a double boiler until liquid. Dissolve the borax in the warmed distilled water and stir the two liquids together until cool. While stirring pierce the capsules and beat the wheatgerm oil into the cream.

To make the cream particularly beneficial to your skin add some crushed herbs to it or substitute juices for the distilled water, such as houseleek, comfrey or marigold.

Avocado nourishing cream

1 tablespoon almond oil
3 tablespoons avocado oil
1 teaspoon beeswax
pinch of borax
1 tablespoon rosewater

Melt the oils and the wax in a double boiler. Dissolve the borax in the rosewater and add to the oils, stirring until cool, rich and creamy.

Simple nourishing cream

1 egg white
2 teaspoons honey
few drops oil of almonds

Beat the egg white and add it to the honey; stir in the oil of almonds.

Moisturizing cream

1 *teaspoon beeswax*
½ *teaspoon vegetable margarine or cocoa butter*
2½ *teaspoons coconut oil*
½ *teaspoon lanolin*
pinch of borax
2 *tablespoons distilled water*

Melt the wax, margarine, oil and lanolin in a double boiler. Dissolve the borax in the warmed water and add it to the oils, beating until the mixture cools.

Cucumber moisturizing cream

1 *teaspoon beeswax*
½ *teaspoon cocoa butter*
2½ *teaspoons coconut oil*
1 *teaspoon lanolin*
pinch of borax
2 *tablespoons cucumber juice*

Proceed as for previous cream.

Lily and marshmallow cream

1 *cup distilled water*
1 *tablespoon lilybulb powder*
1 *tablespoon marshmallow root powder*
1 *tablespoon honey*
1 *ounce lanolin*
1 *teaspoon rosewater*

Add the water to the powders, stir until combined and simmer for half an hour to form a mucilage. Strain the mucilage and add the honey to it. Melt the lanolin and combine it with the other liquid, and slowly add the rosewater while stirring.

Comfrey cream
2 tablespoons lanolin
3 tablespoons beeswax
3 tablespoons almond oil
pinch of borax
1 tablespoon distilled water
1 tablespoon strong comfrey infusion

Melt the lanolin and wax in the oil and dissolve the borax in the warmed water. Combine the two while slowly stirring in the comfrey infusion.

Herbal moisturizing lotion
1 teaspoon cocoa butter
1 teaspoon lanolin
1 tablespoon almond oil
1 capsule wheatgerm oil
2 teaspoons herbal infusion

Melt all the ingredients except the herbal infusion in a double boiler. Stir in the infusion while cooling the cream.

Lettuce moisturizing lotion
1 head lettuce
1 cup distilled water

Boil the lettuce leaves in the water for about 10 minutes. Leave until cool, then strain and bottle.

Herbal dairy cream
2 *tablespoons heavy cream*
1 *tablespoon herb juice*

Beat together until thick and put up for use.

Rosewater moisture lotion
4 *tablespoons glycerine*
3 *tablespoons rosewater*

Pour into a bottle and shake before use.

 For the body

BATHING

Taking a bath can be turned into a luxurious and deliciously scented event with the help of a few well chosen soaps, herbs and oils.

SOAPS
The most usual cleansing ingredient in taking a bath, apart from hot water, is a cake of a soap, and there are several ways of making them at home without using animal fats or tallow. One of my favorites is a rich one, particularly suited to cleansing the face with a complexion brush, as described on page 30.

Before you start making your own soap, a few words of warning: Be very careful when using lye: if even a speck of it gets onto your skin, wash immediately with cold water, lemon juice or vinegar or you may get a horribly painful burn. Always wear rubber gloves to avoid this.

Try not to breathe the fumes from the soda when mixing it with the water or the oils—it could damage your lungs!

Never use aluminum, tin, or foil containers, because

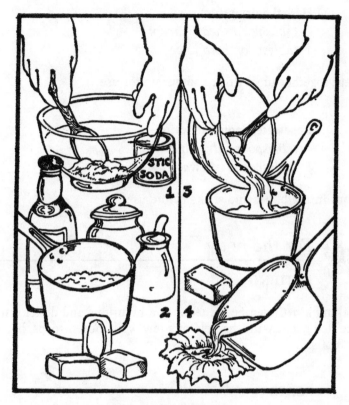

Making your own soap

the lye will gradually eat its way through amidst frothy evil smelling bubbles!

Bearing these words of caution in mind, making soap is quite straightforward.

Rich complexion soap

1 cup water
2 level tablespoons lye (caustic soda)
1½ cups almond or olive oil
½ cup coconut oil
2 teaspoons glycerine or honey

Put the water into a glass or ceramic bowl and, wearing rubber gloves, carefully measure the lye and slowly stir it into the water using a wooden spoon, until dissolved. Melt the coconut and almond oils with the glycerine in an enamel saucepan until warm. The lye solution will have gotten quite hot so leave it until just warm before pouring it slowly, while stirring, into the oils. Keep stirring until the mixture thickens (this could take up to 15 minutes, so do persevere). If the mixture congeals just place the saucepan in a pan of hot water and stir it until it gets back to a good pouring consistency.

Line three plastic or wooden boxes, about 2½" × 3" and 1" deep, with pieces of polythene (to help lift the hardened soap from the molds) and pour the thickened mixture into them. Put the boxes on a tray, cover with a piece of cardboard, wrap in a towel or blanket and put it in a warm dry place until set. (This should happen in 24 hours but sometimes it takes longer.) When set, lift the soap from the molds, peel off the polythene, wrap it in wax paper and store in a cool dry place until quite hard (at least two weeks). This makes a lovely pure white soap.

Simple bath soap

1 cup water
4 heaping tablespoons lye (caustic soda)
2 tablespoons olive oil
2 tablespoons coconut oil
2 tablespoons vegetable margarine

Proceed exactly as before, substituting the margarine for the glycerine or honey.

If you want to add color, perfume or nourishing ingredients to your simple soap do so just before pouring the thickened liquid into the molds for setting, and combine thoroughly by stirring. Add a few drops of any essential oils—only two at a time and stir thoroughly—too strong a smell will be off-putting. Try adding a couple of spoonfuls of mashed avocado, strawberry, cucumber, oatmeal, Irish moss (carrageen), ground almonds, chopped fresh herbs or flowers, and a little coloring either to match your bathroom décor or echo the natural color of the extra ingredients or perfume. Try carving the soaps into shapes or engraving your initials into it before you wrap it up to finally harden.

If the idea of using lye frightens you, try making a soap substitute.

Almond soap substitute

2 tablespoons finely ground almonds
2 tablespoons kaolin powder
½ teaspoon borax
few drops oil of almonds

Mix all the ingredients together and use a knob of it instead of soap.

BATH OILS AND SALTS

The only vegetable oil that will make a good dispersing agent is "treated" castor oil—sometimes known as turkey red oil. "Dispersing" means that the drops of oil will mix with the water and soak into the skin while you are in the bath. All the other oils, including untreated castor oil, will float on top of the water and only get onto your skin as you get out of the bath.

Dispersing bath oil

3 teaspoons treated castor oil
1 teaspoon essential oil

Mix the castor oil with whatever essential oils you like, and use 1 teaspoonful per bath.

Floating bath oils
3 *teaspoons untreated castor oil, olive oil, sesame oil,*
    almond oil, avocado oil
1 *teaspoon essential oil*

Mix and use as before.

Bubble bath oil
½ *cup flaked soap*
¾ *cup hot water*
2 *teaspoons witch hazel*
1½ *tablespoons glycerine*
few drops of essential oils

Dissolve the soap in the hot water. Mix the witch hazel, glycerine and essential oils and combine with the soapy water. Pour two tablespoons into the bath before drawing the water.

Bath salts
1 *lb. sodium sesquicarbonate*
2 *teaspoons essential oil*
a few drops of coloring

Mix all the ingredients until well combined. Store in a clear glass jar and add 1 tablespoon to each bath.

BATH BAGS

Cut a piece of cheesecloth about 7 inches square and in the center of it place 3 tablespoons of whatever ingredients you fancy. Gather the corners and the edges of the cheesecloth around the ingredients and tie up with a length of ribbon. Bags can either be hung from the tap (so that water goes through them), swished in the water, or used to scrub the skin.

In addition to any herbal ingredients bags can contain flaked soap or oatmeal. Never try to by-pass making a bag and toss the herbs straight into the water; not only will you emerge covered in bits of greenery, but in time the drain pipe will get clogged.

BATH INFUSIONS

If you prefer you can add a strong infusion of herbs to your bath water instead of using a bag.

Bath vinegar.
Herbal vinegars too are a good addition to a bath. Pour 1 cup of a ready made herb vinegar into the bath water or make up a special one using particular herbs:

> 1 *cup cider vinegar*
> 3 *tablespoons rosemary, pine, fennel or any herbs you like*
> 1 *cup water*

Mix the vinegar and the water and heat it until nearly boiling, add the herbs, cover and steep overnight. Strain before bottling and use 1 cup per bath.

Some of the nicest bath herbs include the ones listed, which you can use in any combination:

> lovage, dandelion, nettle, marigold or calendula, cowslip, pine needles, elderflowers, limeflowers, violet, southernwood, lemon balm, fennel, rosemary, lavender, eucalyptus, chamomile, houseleek, mint, comfrey.

BODY LOTIONS AND TONICS

After bathing you may like to tone up your skin by splashing with a cool lotion. The simplest tonic is cold water—but you could use rosewater, elderflower water, any cold herbal infusions, cologne, floral water, or herbal vinegars, diluted one part vinegar to eight parts water.

Probably one of the very oldest body tonic lotions goes by the name of Queen of Hungary Water, which also serves as a light perfume; for the recipe see page 57 in the Perfume section.

NOURISHING YOUR SKIN

If your skin is rather undernourished or dry and needs feeding, see pages 40 to 43 in the Face section for nourishing and moisturizing creams and lotions.

DUSTING POWDERS

To make your own dusting powders you will need either unscented talcum powder, cornstarch, riceflour or precipitated chalk, in large quantities, and smaller quantities of orrisroot powder, boric acid powder, and an assortment of essential oils, herbal infusions or floral waters.

Unscented dusting powder

1 cup cornstarch
2 tablespoons boric acid
1 cup precipitated chalk

Pulverize the starch in a pestle and mortar and combine it with the other ingredients. Sieve twice before using.

Basic powder for scenting

1 cup riceflour or cornstarch
2 tablespoons boric acid
4 tablespoons orrisroot powder
1 cup talcum or precipitated chalk
essential oils, about a teaspoon

Pulverize the cornstarch and mix with the other powders. Add whatever essential oils you like, either singly or as a subtle combination of smells and stir into the powders until quite absorbed and dry. Sift twice before using.

The orrisroot powder helps to "fix" the smell into the other powders and the boric acid helps make it slightly antiseptic.

If you want to scent your basic powder with floral waters or herbal infusions use 1 teaspoon to each 3 tablespoons of powder and mix and sift until quite dry and scented to your liking.

DEODORANTS

A strong infusion of lovage or goose-grass can be used directly as an underarm deodorant lotion or added to a bathful of water as a general deodorant.

DEPILATORY CREAM

Spurge juice
honey

Mix enough spurge with honey to form a clinging cream. Apply and leave until a test reveals loose hairs. Wash off with warm water or herbal infusion and dust with unscented powder. **Warning:** Do not get the spurge juice anywhere near your eyes or use it on broken skin as it stings horribly!

 ## For sunbathing

Long hours spent in the sun, with nothing to protect the skin from burning, is not only unhealthy but also very aging. Skin needs pampering most when subjected to the elements, particularly the sun, as it can cause more damage than is immediately visible.

Before exposing your skin apply a liberal coating of protective oil or cream, and after sunbathing lavishly rub in lots of moisturizing lotion, for a dry skin will burn much more quickly than a supple, well-fed one. (See pages 40 to 43 for recipes for moisturizing creams and lotions.)

SUNTAN OIL

2 tablespoons lanolin
2 tablespoons sesame oil
6 tablespoons water or herbal infusion

Melt the lanolin with the oil in a double boiler and slowly add the warmed infusion or water.

Citrus sun oil
½ cup sesame oil
6 drops of citronella

Mix, and bottle.

Tea oil
1 tablespoon lanolin
3 tablespoons sesame oil
1 tablespoon coconut oil
4 tablespoons strong cold black tea

Melt the lanolin in the oils in a double boiler. Remove from the heat and stir in the cold tea.

Olive suntan oil
3 tablespoons olive oil
2 tablespoons sesame oil
1 tablespoon cider vinegar
few drops oil of bergamot

Mix all the ingredients together and pour into a bottle.

Sesame oil is about the best to use as protection from sunburn because it actually absorbs a lot of the ultra-violet rays.

The oils mentioned are marvellous if your skin tans fairly readily but should you have a delicate skin either do not sunbathe at all or consult your doctor for advice. (See pages 40 to 43 for recipes for moisturizing creams and lotions.)

If you do get at all sunburned there are several lotions you can wash over your poor red, itchy, hot skin.

Cold tea is surprisingly soothing; so too is a mixture of olive oil and vinegar; infusions of lettuce leaves, chamomile, nettles, sage and cowslip, and houseleek and the juice from a cucumber are especially cooling.

 For hands and nails

NAILS

To strengthen finger nails

Rub pure lanolin into cuticles each night.

Paint nails with white iodine after each immersion into water.

Mix equal parts of castor oil and glycerine and rub into fingertips and cuticles.

Soak fingertips in a strong infusion of dill or horsetail.

To color finger nails

Make a thick paste with henna powder and warm water. Leave on until quite dry, then wash paste off. The nails will then have a pinky tinge to them.

HAND CREAMS

Almond hand cream

⅓ *cup ground almonds*
⅔ *cup milk*
1 *egg yolk*
1 *teaspoon almond oil*

Boil the ground almonds in the milk until they are absorbed. Stir in the beaten egg yolk and re-heat. Cool and add the almond oil.

Hand jelly

1 *tablespoon glycerine*
1 *tablespoon arrowroot*
½ *cup orangeflower water*

Warm the glycerine in a double boiler and slowly add the arrowroot to form a paste. Add the warmed orangeflower water and continue stirring until the mixture clears.

Cocoa hand cream

2 *tablespoons cocoa butter*
2 *tablespoons beeswax*
2 *tablespoons almond oil*

Melt the butter and the wax in a double boiler and stir in the oil. Put up for use.

Quince hand cream

1 *teaspoon quince seeds*
1 *cup hot water*
1 *tablespoon witch hazel*
2 *tablespoons glycerine*

Make a mucilage with the quince seeds and the hot water; strain when ready and combine it with the other ingredients.

BARRIER CREAMS

Hand barrier cream
1 ounce or about 2 tablespoons lanolin
1 tablespoon beeswax
½ cup mineral oil
⅓ cup distilled water or herbal infusion
pinch of borax

Melt the lanolin and the wax and combine with the mineral oil. Dissolve the borax in the water and stir into the wax and oil solution. Put up when thick and cooled.

Egg paste barrier cream
1 egg yolk
1 tablespoon sunflower oil
kaolin powder

Mix the egg yolk and the sunflower oil with enough kaolin powder to form a paste. Rub on hands before doing heavy work.

To clean stained hands:
1 tablespoon of sunflower oil mixed with
1 tablespoon of sugar
Rub the mixture into your hands until clean and rinse off with water.
or
1 tablespoon sesame oil mixed with
1 tablespoon lemon juice
1 tablespoon honey

Use as before.

Stained elbows can be cleaned most effectively by leaning them in a halved lemon each for at least 5 minutes.

For the feet

FOOT BATHS

To soothe tired or sore feet soak them in a bowl containing a couple of handfuls of nettle leaves, rosemary, lavender, mint or horsetail, covered in boiling water, but don't put your feet in until the water cools to a bearable temperature. Sea salt in hot water can also be very soothing.

If on a cold and miserably wet day you need warming up, a pinch of crushed mustard seed or powder added to hot water will soon make you feel cozy.

NAIL STRENGTHENERS AND NOURISHING CREAMS

These can be the same as those you use on your hands.

ROUGH SKIN REMOVER

> 2 *tablespoons yogurt*
> 1 *tablespoon herbal or cider vinegar*

Mix the two together and cover your feet with it, rubbing it well into the hard skinned parts. Leave on for about 10 minutes and rub it off followed by a warm water bath.

COOLING FOOT POWDER

> ½ *teaspoon menthol*
> 1 *teaspoon witch hazel*
> 1 *teaspoon boric acid powder*
> 1 *cup precipitated chalk*

Dissolve the menthol in the witch hazel and combine with the boric acid powder and the chalk. Sift twice and use.

Floral waters and colognes

The simplest fragrances to make at home are floral waters. You just add about 15 drops of essential oil to a pint of distilled water and shake the bottle. The most versatile of these waters are, rosewater, orangeflower water, and lavender water: but the possibilities are endless and are just a question of personal preference.

More complex smells are produced by blending carefully measured amounts of oils with pure alcohol or vodka.

FLORAL WATERS

Lavender water

10 drops of lavender
1 tablespoon rosewater
3 tablespoons vodka or alcohol

Melissa water

¼ cup lemon balm leaves, crushed
1 teaspoon lemon peel, grated
¼ teaspoon allspice
½ cup vodka or alcohol
¾ cup distilled water

Mix all together except the water, steep for a week and strain before adding the water.

Florida water

¼ cup vodka or alcohol
7 drops oil of lavender
10 drops oil of bergamot
4 drops oil of cloves

Hungary water
1 *tablespoon mint leaves, fresh*
1 *tablespoon rosemary, fresh*
¼ *cup vodka or alcohol*
½ *cup rosewater*
grated peel of ¼ of lemon and orange

Mix all together, pour into a bottle and steep for a week. Strain before using.

COLOGNES

Eau de Cologne
4 *tablespoons rose petals, fresh*
½ *cup vodka or alcohol*
1 *tablespoon basil, fresh*
1 *tablespoon peppermint, fresh*
2 *tablespoons lemon peel*
2 *tablespoons orange peel*
1 *cup boiling water*

Soak the rose petals in the alcohol for a week. Crush all the leaves and grate the peel and steep in the hot water. Strain both liquids and combine in a bottle.

Bay rum cologne
1 *teaspoon rum*
a few drops oil of bay
1½ *tablespoons distilled water*
2½ *tablespoons vodka or alcohol*

Mix all the ingredients and pour into a bottle.

For sleep

The most natural cosmetic of all and the best pick-me-up is our beauty sleep. So if you have any trouble actually getting to sleep try having a delicious hot, sleep-inducing herbal tea or tisane and tucking a herb cushion under your pillow.

Try a sleep-inducing herbal tea

HERBAL TEAS

Warm a china or glass teapot with hot water. (Glass is particularly pretty as you can see the leaves or flowers floating in a pale liquid.) If you are using dried herbs put 1 teaspoonful for each cup and 1 extra for the pot. If using fresh herbs put 3 teaspoons per cup and 3 for the pot, crushing the leaves before use. Fresh herbs give a much lighter, fresher tasting tea than the dried ones. Put the herbs in the teapot and cover with boiling water; leave to steep for at least 5 minutes before pouring.

Or try this Russian recipe, for a change.

> *2 teaspoons valerian*
> *1 cup milk*
> *1 teaspoon cider vinegar*
> *3 teaspoons honey*
> *3 teaspoons vodka*

Crush the valerian and boil it in the milk for several minutes, strain off the pieces and mix the liquid with the other ingredients and drink while hot.

SLEEP-INDUCING HERBAL PILLOWS

Having had a lovely hot drink rest your head on a cushion of sweet smelling herbs, almost sure to give you pleasant dreams. Make a bag from two pieces of cloth—about 6 inches by 10 inches—and fill it with any of the following tea herbs or any other aromatics you like the smell of. Hops are a good basic filler for a pillow, with a few spoonfuls of herbs for scent; in fact these and bay leaves are two age-old remedies against sleeplessness.

Relaxing and sleep-inducing herbs
Clover, cowslip, hops, mignonette, peppermint, lime, chamomile, sage, lemon balm, catnip, valerian, lettuce and bergamot (monarda).

Other fragrant additions to a pillow include:
cloves, cinnamon, allspice, lemon and orange peel, lavender, thyme, orrisroot and pine needles.

THREE

Gathering, drying and storing herbs

So that your cosmetics are fully beneficial to you in their herbal content, you will need to know the best ways of harvesting, drying and storing the various plants, be they leaves, seeds, flowers or roots and how to use them to best advantage. Even if you buy ready-dried herbs you will still need to know the best ways to keep them.

If you gather your plants in the wrong way or at the wrong time a lot of their value will be lost. It is important too that you know just which part of the plant you will eventually need; for this see the recipes and the ABC of ingredients.

Harvesting from the garden should present few if any problems. In the countryside do be sure that you are not picking any rare or locally protected plants. Try to learn about the growth habits of the plants you are likely to need, so that you know exactly what you are doing when collecting, and keep a wary eye for the ravages of weedkillers and pesticides—be sure your plants have not been contaminated.

The best time for collecting is the late morning on a sunny and warm day. Never pick plants that are at all wet (this includes dew!) and then only gather the insect-free ones. Do not stuff them into a bag but gently lay them in a flat basket; gather a few at a time—the slightest crushing or bruising will rob your collection of some of its valuable

ingredients—and do not pick more than you can easily deal
with at one time.

If you are gathering *leaves* pick them when the flowers on the plant are still in bud and do not strip off too many
from each plant as it may reduce its strength—try to pick the
young leaves and shoots.

When gathering *flowers* nip them off the stem just

before they open, so that the valuable oils do not have a chance to escape.

Sometimes you will need the whole of the plant which is above the soil—leaves and stems—this is what is known as "the herb"—cut these at ground level just after flowering. You might need the *whole plant including the root* in which case lift it when the plant is in flower by loosening the soil around the roots and pulling it up gently; wash off any soil left on the roots and dry them with a cloth.

When you need the *root only* lift them in autumn when they are mature and rinse off any soil, cut off any fibrous growth and dry with a cloth.

Seeds you should gather when ripe: cut the whole seeding flower head from the plant, tie a paper bag over it and hang it upside down in a dry place until the seeds fall out; sometimes you will have to rub off the outer seed casing by hand.

You may be fortunate enough to have an empty room which you can devote to drying plants, which for best results should be kept well shaded and at a temperature of at least 90°F for the first day of drying and then at an even 70°F. But there is no real need to go to such extremes. A warm spot in the attic, in the kitchen pantry or the oven will work just as well for drying small quantities.

The only exception to the shade rule are roots, which should ideally be dried in full sun. Whole plants you can hang up in bunches from a piece of string across a room, but leaves and flowers will need spreading out thinly on wire racks, blotting paper or in cardboard boxes (without the lid on). Be sure to turn them daily and check for signs of mold.

Most important—label all plants you are drying and keep each different kind separately.

All dried plant material must also be stored properly for it to stay useful. Properly dried flowers will look and feel papery, leaves will be crisp and crumbly and roots and stems will snap easily between fingers. Ideally you should store dried herbs in small opaque pots with cork lids (if you use clear jars do be sure to keep them in the dark). You could keep your collection in little brown bags in a dry place—but do not be tempted to use big bags because the herbs will not be able to breathe and may eventually rot.

FOUR

An ABC of herbal terms for cosmetics

Processes and terms

There are various processes and terms mentioned in the recipes which you need to understand to be able to make your cosmetics properly; they may seem a little complicated at first but once you've read and made them you will see just how easy it really is.

Decoction: Usually made of sliced plant root boiled in water. Put 1 tablespoon of root into 2 cups of water in an enamel or stainless steel pan and, with the lid almost covering it, boil the water until it is reduced by $1/3$: this should take about half an hour. The remaining liquid is then a decoction.

Essence: Solely for external use. Add 3 tablespoons of essential oil to 2 cups of alcohol (or vodka or surgical spirit) or vinegar.

Essential oil (or volatile oil): Found mainly in the flowers of plants, though also in the fruit, stem, root or leaf. The simplest method of getting essential oils from citrus fruits is by squeezing the peel: technically this is known as "expression." Two other methods used chiefly for obtaining "flower" essential oils are known as "distillation" and "solvent extraction" —neither of which can be done satisfactorily at home. The oils can be readily bought from many herbalists or ordered through a chemist.

Extract: Fill a small screw-top jar full of fresh crushed aromatic leaves and add ½ cup of alcohol, wine vinegar or oil. Leave the jar and its contents to stand for a week, strain the liquid into another jar and add more leaves and let it stand for another week. Continue until the liquid has absorbed the smell of the plant.

Herbal oils: Crush or blend the leaves and stems of fresh herbs with a pestle and mortar or blender and put 2 tablespoons into a 1 cup screw-top jar. Add 1 tablespoon of white wine vinegar or cider vinegar and fill ⅓ with corn, sunflower or olive oil. Put on the lid and shake the jar. Stand it in a warm and sunny place for about three weeks. During this time shake the jar at least twice a day. Strain and repeat the process with fresh herbs as many times as necessary until the oil has absorbed the smell of the herbs. If there is no place sunny enough for the jar to stand, unscrew the top by one turn, stand it in a pan of water and heat it until the contents of the jar are warmed; repeat this every day for at least three weeks.

Herbal vinegar: Crush or blend 1–2 tablespoons fresh herbs, put them in a screw-top jar and add ½ cup of white wine vinegar or cider vinegar. Put on the lid and shake the jar; leave it in a warm place and shake or stir it every other day. After two weeks check the fragrance; if not strong enough strain out the old herbs, replace with new ones and repeat the process.

Infusion or tisane: *Standard infusion:* Pour 1 cup of boiling water over 4 tablespoons of dried herbal leaves or flowers and leave to steep for anything between ½ hour and 2 hours. *Weak infusion:* 2 tablespoons herbs to 1 cup water. *Strong infusion:* 8 tablespoons herbs to 1 cup water. Keep the steeping herbs covered until cool and ready to be strained. Never boil the herbs in the water.

Liniment or embrocation: Add soothing herbs to melted lard or oil such as olive oil in a ratio of 1 to 4 and simmer for 20–30 minutes. Strain, cool and cover. Use to rub on sprains and stiff or aching joints.

Maceration: Soak crushed seeds etc. with water for at least 2 hours.

Mucilage: Basically a sticky substance exuded by plants such as resins and gums, or a decoction or maceration of roots, seeds or leaves, used as a stabilizing agent in creams.

Steeping: This simply means leaving a "brew" to stand for a while until the beneficial ingredients in a plant have been absorbed by the liquid it is soaking in.

Tincture: Put 2 tablespoons of dried herbs or powdered resin in a screw-top jar and cover it with ½ cup of alcohol (or vodka or surgical spirit) or wine vinegar; cover and leave it in a warm place for a couple of weeks, shaking it regularly.

Ingredients

Alcohol: Pure alcohol is not always available. See *Vodka*.

Allspice: (*Pimenta officinalis*) Usually used in powder form. Smells of cloves, juniper berries, cinnamon and pepper.

Almond: (*Prunus dulcis*) Ground almonds are used in creams. The "cake" left after extracting the oil from the nut kernels is used as a soap substitute.

Almond oil: Clear, pale yellow and odorless, fine texture. Much used in creams.

Alum: Fine white granules, resembling powdered sugar; used in astringent lotions.

Angelica: (*Angelica archangelica*) Dried root added to bath bags.

Apple: A naturally acid fruit; the juice and fruit are used in face masks.

Apple vinegar: see *Cider vinegar*.

Arrowroot: (*Maranta arundinacea*) A starchy white powder used for thickening lotions.

Avocado: (*Persea americana*) A tropical fruit which provides a rich nourishing oil. Used in cosmetics. Use mashed fruit in face masks.

Balm: see *Lemon balm*.

Balsam: Gummy aromatic resins from a number of plants and trees. See *Benzoin* and *Tragacanth*.

Barley: (*Hordeum vulgare*) A decoction of pearl barley seeds is used as a face lotion.

Basil: (*Ocimum basilicum*) Aromatic herb: use infusion of leaves for skin tonics and baths.

Bay: (*Laurus nobilis*) Add dried leaves to pillows.

Bay oil: (*Pimenta acris*) Volatile oil.

Beer: A useful body-giving hair-setting lotion.

Beeswax: (*Cera alba*) Used in creams: emulsifies if used with borax.

Benzoin: (*Styrax benzoin*) A balsamic resin which will only dissolve in alcohol.

Bergamot: (*Citrus bergamia*) Provides a volatile oil used mostly in perfumes and colognes; not to be confused with the herb.

Bergamot: (*Monarda didyma*) An aromatic herb, dried leaves of which are used as tisanes.

Blackberry: (*Rubus fruticosus*) Leaves and roots are used as strong infusions for baths and astringent lotions.

Borax: A white powder used as an emulsifier with beeswax; has mildly antiseptic action in lotions.

Boric acid: (*boracic acid*) Either powder or crystal used in lotions, creams and powders.

Bread: Charred bread mixed with peppermint oil can be used as a tooth cleaning paste.

Buttermilk: Used as a base for face masks or a cleanser.

Calendula: (*Calendula officinalis*) Infusion of the whole plant above ground can be added to creams and lotions: soothing and healing. Known as pot-marigold; other marigolds may be substituted.

Carrageen: see *Irish moss*

Camphor: (*Cinnamonum camphora*) Not moth balls. Usually sold as spirit of camphor; used in skin tonics; has healing and soothing effect.

Cardamon: (*Elettaria cardamonum*) Seeds are added to pillows.

Carrot: Grated root and juice used in face masks.

Cassie: (*Acacia farnesiana*) Volatile oil.

Castor oil: (*Ricinus communis*) A rich clear oil. When "treated" it is known as Turkey red oil, which will disperse in water, so making it a good agent for volatile oils in preparing fragrant bath oils.

Catnip: *(Nepeta cataria)* An infusion of leaves can be used as a tisane or hair rinse.

Caustic soda or lye: (*sodium hydroxide*) White crystals used in soap making.

Cedarwood: (*Juniperus virginiana*) Volatile oil.

Chalk: see *precipitated chalk.*

Chamomile: (*Matricaria chamomilla*) Infusions of the flowers and leaves are used as tisanes, hair and complexion washes.

Cider vinegar: Apple vinegar used diluted as a hair rinse or bath additive. A good base for herbal vinegars.

Cinnamon: (*Cinnamomum zeylanicum*) Volatile oil or powder; can be added to colognes and pillows.

Citronella: (*Cymbopogon nardus*) Volatile oil.

Cleavers: (*Galium aparine*) Goosegrass. An infusion of leaves and stems makes a good deodorizing lotion.

Clover: (*Trifolium pratense*) Use an infusion of flowers as a tisane.

Cloves: (*Eugenia aromatica*) Aromatic spice; used crushed in powders; the volatile oil is used in perfuming.

Cocoa butter: (*Theobroma cacao*) A yellowish white waxy fat used in creams.

Coconut oil: (*Cocos nucifera*) A waxy white oil used in creams.

Cologne: (*Eau-de-cologne*) A fragrant liquid made from alcohol and various aromatic oils.

Coloring: Use any vegetable food coloring agents.

Coltsfoot: (*Tussilago farfara*) Use an infusion of the leaves as an eye bath.

Columbine: (*Aquilegia vulgaris*) Infusion of leaves as a hair rinse.

Comfrey: (*Symphytum officinale*) A decoction of the roots make a soothing and healing addition to body creams and sunburn lotions; leaves will do the same but to a lesser degree.

Cornflower: (*Centaurea cyanus*) Use an infusion of the flowers as an eyebath or for a steam facial.

Corn oil: (*Zea mays*) A clear pale yellow oil used in creams.

Cornstarch: (*Zea mays*) A white powder used as a base for dusting powders.

Cowslip: (*Primula veris*) Flowers; addition to bath bags and face masks.

Cream: Light or heavy as a base for nourishing face masks. Sour cream is good for dry skin.

Cucumber: (*Cucumis sativus*) Mildly astringent and soothing: juices used in lotions, masks and creams.

Dandelion: (*Taraxacum officinale*) An infusion of the leaves and flowers can be used in skin washes and face masks.

Dill: (*Anethum graveolens*) Seeds and leaves can be added to pillows.

Distilled water: Purified water. Use in all creams and lotions. Do not use rainwater unless you can be certain that it is pure.

Decoction: see page 69.

Eggs: Yolks and whites are used in face masks and hair conditioners.

Elderflowers: (*Sambucus nigra*) Flowers used in creams and lotions.

Embrocation: see page 70.

Essence: see page 69.

Essential oil: See page 69.

Eucalyptus: (*Eucalyptus globulus*) Volatile oil.

Extract: see page 70.

Fennel: (*Feoniculum vulgare*) Infusions of seeds used as eye-bath, skin lotions or added to steam facials.

Flaked soap: Grated soap used as an emulsifying agent; also in shampoo.

Floral waters: Add 12 drops of essence to 2 cups of distilled water. Can be used as hair rinses, bath additives and fragrant body lotions.

Fuller's earth: A grayish powder used as a base for face masks.

Glycerine: A syrupy, sweet, colorless liquid used in creams, lotions and soaps; obtained from vegetable oils by saponification, from sugar and by a modern synthetic process. (Also from animal fats so be sure to get the right one; if you can't, try mixing honey with water as an alternative.)

Henna: (*Lawsonia inermis*) A khaki-colored powder used as hair, nail and skin dye.

Herbal oil: see page 70.

Honey: Nourishing and softening; can be added to creams, lotions, masks and soaps.

Hops: (*Humulus lupulus*) Dried flowers used in pillows.

Horseradish: (*Cochlearia armoracia*) Grated root is used in bleaching masks.

Horsetail: (*Equisetum arvense etc.*) Infusion of the whole plant above ground used for strengthening nails or rinsing hair.

Houseleek: *(Sempervivum tectorum)* The leaves have astrigent properties: used in creams, lotions, bath bags and masks.

Iodine: Extracted from seaweed: paint onto nails to strengthen.

Irish moss: (*Chondrus crispus*) Carrageen. A seaweed used as an emolient mucilage in creams.

Jasmine: Volatile oil from flowers of many plants of the jasmine family.

Kaolin: A fine white powder used as a base for masks.

Lady's mantle: (*Alchemilla vulgaris*) Infusion of the whole plant above ground is used in lotions and creams and steam facials.

Lanolin: A thick sticky fat from sheep's wool; used in moisturizing skin creams.

Lavender: (*Lavandula officinalis etc.*) Flowers and leaves produce volatile oils. Can be used in breath fresheners or foot baths.

Lemon: (*Citrus limonium*) The peel produces the volatile oil. Juice can be used in skin creams, lotions, masks and hair rinses.

Lemon balm: (*Melissa officinalis*) A fragrant herb used in colognes; infusions of leaves used as an anti-freckle face wash.

Lemon verbena: (*Lippia citriodora*) Infusion of leaves used as a hair rinse.

Lettuce: A decoction of the leaves can be used as a light moisturizer. Leaves eaten last thing at night will promote sleep.

Lily: (*Lilium candidum*) Dried bulb used in face creams.

Lime: (*Citrus aurantifolia*) Volatile oil from peel. Juice used in face masks.

Lime: (*Tilia europaea*) Infusion of flowers used as hair rinse, addition to bath water or bag or drunk as a tisane.

Liquid Paraffin: see *Mineral oil*

Liniment: see page 70.

Lovage: (*Levisticum officinalis*) Aromatic herb: decoction of root or infusion of leaves used as a deodorizing lotion.

Maceration: see page 70.

Margarine: Must be totally vegetable: used in lotions and soaps.

Marigold: see *Calendula*.

Marshmallow: (*Althaea officinalis*) A mucilage of the root is added to moisturizing lotions and creams.

Melissa: see *lemon balm*.

Menthol: Strongly scented colorless crystals obtained from the leaves of various kinds of mint.

Mignonette: (*Reseda lutea*) Leaves used for making tisanes.

Milk: Dried; added as a thickener to face masks. Fresh; used as a cleanser.

Mineral oil: Clear oil used in barrier creams or bath oils.

Mint: (*Mentha viridis*) Infusion of leaves added to bath bags or water.

Mucilage: see page 71.

Mullein: (*Verbascum thapsus*) Infusion of flowers used as a hair rinse.

Mustard: (*Sinapsis alba*) Powdered seeds used in a foot bath.

Nasturtium: (*Tropaeolum majus*) Infusion of leaves added to steam facials.

Neroli: (*Citrus aurantium*) Volatile oil from orange flowers.

Nettle: (*Urtica dioica*) Infusion of leaves used as a hair rinse, bath additive or astringent lotion.

Nutmeg: (*Myristica fragrans*) Volatile oil. Powdered nut used in fragrant waters and powders.

Oats: (*Avena sativa*) Ground seeds of "meal" used in masks and bath bags.

Oils: see individual names.

Olive oil: (*Olea europaea*) A polyunsaturated oil used in skin creams.

Orange: (*Citrus sinensis*) Juice used in face masks. Peel used in colognes and pillows.

Orange flower: see *Neroli*.

Orange flower water: see *Floral waters*.

Orrisroot: (*Iris florentina*) Dried powdered root, slightly violet-scented; used in dusting powders, pillows and dry shampoos.

Parsley: (*Petroselinum crispum*) Infusion of leaves used as an eye bath or added to creams and lotions. Crushed leaves used in masks or as a breath freshener.

Patchouli: (*Pogostemon patchouli*) Volatile oil.

Peach: (*Prunus persica*) Juice or mashed fruit can be added to masks.

Peanut oil: (*Arachis hypogaea*) Used in creams and lotions.

Peppermint: (*Mentha piperita*) Volatile oil. Infusion of leaves is mildly astringent. Can be drunk as a tisane. Dried leaves can be added to pillows.

Pine: (*Pinus sylvestris*) Volatile oil. Crushed leaves can be added to pillows or bath bags.

Potato: (*Solanum tuberosum*) Juice and slices can be used as cleanser or added to masks.

Precipitated chalk: White powder used as a base for dusting powders.

Privet: (*Ligustrum vulgare*) Infusion of leaves used as a hair color.

Porridge oats: see *Oats*.

Quince: (*Cydonia oblonga*) A decoction of the seeds makes a mucilage used in creams and lotions. The juice is used in hair coloring.

Rhubarb: (*Rheum rhaponticum*) A decoction of the roots or stalks is used for lightening hair.

Rice flour: (*Oryza sativa*) White powder used as a base for masks or dusting powder.

Rose: (*Rosa*) Petals produce volatile oils. (Use only old-fashioned or very fragrant modern kinds.)

Rose hip: Infusion used as an eyebath or powdered in a mask.

Rosemary: (*Rosmarinus officinalis*) Infusions of leaves and flowers used as hair rinses, and skin lotions or added to bath water. Dried; added to bath bags or pillows.

Rosewater: see *Floral waters*.

Rum: Used as the spirit base for Bay rum oil.

Safflower: (*Carthamus tinctorius*) Polyunsaturated oil used in creams.

Sage: (*Salvia officinalis*) Chew fresh leaves to clean teeth. Use an infusion of leaves as a hair rinse and color.

Salad Burnet: (*Poterium sanguisorba*) Add crushed leaves to an astringent mask.

Salt: see *Sea salt*.

Sandalwood: (*Santalum album*) Volatile oil.

Sea salt: Added to baths and for cleaning teeth.

Sesame oil: (*Sesamum orientale*) Polyunsaturated oil, particularly good in suntan preparations.

Soap: Mixture of vegetable oils, lye and water.

Soapwort: *(Saponaria officinalis)* Decoction or roots or infusion of leaves gives a lathery cleansing liquid. Can be used as a shampoo or added to bath bags.

Sodium sesquicarbonate: Water-softening crystals used in making bath salts.

Southernwood: (*Artemisia abrotanum*) Infusion used as a hair rinse.

Spurge: (*Euphorbia lathyris*) Juice used as a depilatory.

Starch: see *Cornstarch*

Strawberry: (*Fragaria*) Juices are mildly astringent and can be used to clean and tone the skin. The powdered root can be used as a toothpowder.

Steeping: see page 71.

Sugar: Icing sugar used for making pastilles. Granulated used for setting lotions.

Sunflower oil: *(Helianthus annus)* A polyunsaturated oil used in skin creams.

Surgical spirit: Used in astringent lotions.

Talcum: A finely ground talc used as a dusting powder.

Tansy: *(Tanacetum vulgare)* Decoction of leaves and flowers used as an anti-freckle lotion.

Teas: see page 59, 123, and 134ff.

Thyme: *(Thymus, various)* Infusion of leaves and used as face lotion and steam facial. Dried leaves used in bath bags and pillows.

Tincture: see page 71.

Tisanes: see teas on page 59, 123, and 134ff; also page 70.

Tomato: *(Lycopersicum esculentum)* Mashed as a face mask.

Tragacanth: *(Astragalus gummifer)* Used where a mucilage is needed. Stand the granules in water to dissolve.

Turkey red oil: see *Castor oil.*

Valerian: *(Valeriana officinalis)* Dried leaves added to pillows.

Verbena: see *Lemon verbena.*

Vinegar: see *Cider vinegar* and *Wine vinegar.*

Violets: *(Viola odorata)* Volatile oil.

Vodka: Use as alcohol substitute in astringent lotions and colognes.

Volatile oil: see *Essential oil* on page 69.

Walnut: *(Juglans nigra or regia)* Skins used in hair dye.

Water: see *Distilled water.*

Watercress: *(Nasturtium officinale)* Juices good for clearing blemishes. Add to masks or creams.

Wax: see *Beeswax.*

Wheatgerm oil: Rich nourishing oil used in creams.

Wine: White wine used in making a hair lightener.

Wine vinegar: Used in preparing herbal oils.

Witch hazel: (*Hamamelis virginiana*) Astringent spirit, used in lotions.

Yarrow: (*Achillea millefolium*) Infusion of the whole plant above ground used as a hair rinse or crushed and added to masks.

Yeast: Either fresh, dried or tablets, dissolved and added to masks.

Yogurt: Natural yogurt used as a base for masks, also alone as a cleanser.

*Herbs for Cooking,
Cleaning, Canning and
Sundry Household Chores*

Contents
Herbs for Cooking, Cleaning, Canning and Sundry Household Chores

ONE

Alphabetical list of herbs for the household

There are many herbs mentioned in the following list that can be found growing wild in the countryside. The fact that they grow wild is not a license to pick or to remove all you need. This list will help you recognize them in their natural habitat and indicates how best you can reproduce these conditions in your own garden, ensuring sturdy healthy plants.

The following points should be remembered:

1. The conservation of wild plants is important to the countryside. Indiscriminate picking, or trampling, will cause eventual extinction. Many are protected under state conservation guidelines.

2. Flowers, leaves and berries should only be picked when it is clear that by doing so no permanent damage will result.

3. It is essential to identify herbs picked from the wild correctly before preparing them for culinary or medicinal use.

4. Finally, unknown to the picker, the wild plants may have been subjected to chemical sprays blown from neighboring fields or, if by the roadside, to constant fumes from passing traffic. It is much safer to grow your own plants.

For full information about cultivating herbs, see *Choosing, Planting and Cultivating Herbs*, also by Philippa Back, vol. 2 in the Living With Herbs Series (Keats Publishing, Inc., 1977).

Angelica

ANGELICA ARCHANGELICA

A biennial growing up to 6 feet (180cm) high, angelica has thick hollow stems and large fragrant leaves. Honey-scented greenish-white flowers appear from June to August. It can be found growing wild along river banks and damp meadows, but the flavor is best when the plant is grown in the garden.

To cultivate: Plant in moist, rich, partly shaded area. Allow 2 feet between plants. Sow seeds immediately after they ripen on the flower head (August). Take root cuttings in autumn.

Parts used: roots, leaves, leaf stalks, young stems and seeds.

Time to pick: leaves, leaf stalks and stems throughout growing season but before flowering, seeds in the autumn, gather roots in the second year.

Use leaves, fresh or dried, for flavoring fruit salads and drinks. Add leaf stalks, stems or roots to jams and jellies and when cooking tart fruits—this cuts down the amount of sugar required. Candied stems and stalks are used for cake decoration and in ice cream.

Medicinally, angelica is good for the digestion, for coughs, colds and as a syrup for sore throats. Use externally as a compress or ointment to stop itching and soothe the skin.

Barberry

BERBERIS VULGARIS

A deciduous bushy shrub, barberry grows 3–8 feet (90–160cm) high. The pale green leaves are oval shaped and the stems have sharp thorns. Small pale yellow flowers appear in June followed in August and September by clusters of bright red berries, each berry about one-half inch (1¼ cm) long. It can be found growing wild in hedges and copses.

To cultivate: Propagate in October by cuttings or layer young shoots from the lower branches. Plant out the following autumn. Seed sown in a sheltered spot in autumn will germinate in spring.

Parts used: the berries.

Time to pick: October. Berries must be absolutely ripe before gathering.

Use to make jelly and pickles to accompany savory dishes. Use candied berries to decorate sweet dishes.
Medicinally a syrup of the berries makes an effective remedy for sore throats.

Basil

OCIMUM BASILICUM

All varieties are annuals; sweet and opal basil grow 1–2 feet (30–60cm) high, bush basil grows up to 1 foot (30cm). Sweet basil has smooth dark green leaves; the opal has purple leaves, and the bush basil leaves are small and rather pale. The flowers are white. It cannot be found growing wild.

To cultivate: Begin opal varieties indoors, put out in June, 8 inches apart, in sunny, sheltered spot with moist but well-drained soil. Pinch centers to strengthen. Bush variety can be grown in containers: sow seeds in March, thin to 2 plants per 4-inch pot. Pinch to encourage fullness.

Parts used: the leaves.

Time to pick: from June onwards.

Use mainly as a seasoning herb. Add to salads, egg and tomato dishes, mushrooms, pasta sauce and vinegar.

Plants in the house act as insect repellent.

Medicinally, basil infusion is a mild laxative.

Borage

BORAGO OFFICINALIS

A hardy annual, borage grows 1½ feet (45cm) high with large coarse leaves which are rough and prickly. The star-shaped flowers are bright blue. It is normally grown in the garden but it can occasionally be found as a garden escape on waste land. It re-seeds itself freely.

To cultivate: Sow seeds in ground in late spring and mid-summer for successive harvests. Grows quickly in any soil.

Parts used: young leaves and flowers.

Time to pick: throughout the growing season.

Use young leaves in salads, pickles, as a cooked vegetable and to give a cucumber flavor to summer drinks.
Use the flowers in salads and, candied, for decoration.

Calendula (Pot-Marigold)

CALENDULA OFFICINALIS

A hardy annual growing to 1–2 feet (30–60 cm). The leaves are thick and lance-shaped. The flowers, a bright orange yellow, bloom all summer long. Cannot be found growing wild but is an easy plant to grow in the garden or in a container. Related to plant commonly known in America as marigold, which can often be substituted.

To cultivate: Sow seed freely in late spring, full sun, in July for fall crop. Thin to 12 inches.

Parts used: flower petals and leaves.

When to pick: leaves throughout the season and petals when flowers are fully open.

Use the flower petals in broths, salads and sauces, with eggs and cheese. Add to summer drinks.

Medicinally, a lotion made with petals is for sprains and an ointment for sunburn and chapped lips or hands. An infusion of the leaves makes a soothing footbath, and a petal oil is for skin complaints.

Coltsfoot

TUSSILAGO FARFARA

A low-growing hardy perennial, colts-foot has long creeping roots and flowers which grow up to 2 feet (60cm) high. The stalked fragrant gray-green leaves are hoof-shaped and covered on the underside with white woolly hairs. These can grow quite large in places and appear only after the flowers have died down. The round bright yellow drooping flower heads bloom one to each stem. A very common wild plant, it can be found in moist and dry places growing in poor, rather heavy soils.

To cultivate: sow seed in April or May in flowering position and thin to 1 foot apart. Divide plants in autumn.

Once established it is difficult to contain and should only be grown on a patch of waste ground.

Parts used: leaves and flowers.

When to pick: flowers in spring, leaves when small, in early summer.

Use fresh young leaves in fritters with egg and cheese dishes. Use the flowers to make wine.

Medicinally, an infusion of dried or fresh leaves is taken for coughs and colds. Candy or syrup made from the leaves is used for the same purpose.

Dandelion

TARAXACUM OFFICINALE

A hardy perennial with the flower stems growing up to 1 foot (30cm) high. The sharply toothed leaves form flat rosettes on the ground. The fleshy hollow stem carries a single bright yellow flower. A very common plant, dandelion grows wild almost everywhere, and unless you wish to have a more succulent-leafed variety, there is little need to cultivate it.

To cultivate: sow seed in April in an unused patch of garden in a shady spot. For best results do not cut until it is well established.

Parts used: leaves, roots and flowers.

Time to pick: gather leaves throughout the growing season. Dig up the roots in spring or autumn.

Use young leaves in salads, as a green vegetable and to make dandelion tea. Use the flowers for making wine and the roots as a coffee substitute.

Medicinally, the infusion helps to ease stiff joints and provides a diuretic drink.

Dill

ANETHUM GRAVEOLENS

A hardy annual, dill grows up to 3 feet (90cm) high. Very finely divided leaves grow from a thick stem and tiny yellow flowers appear in July and August. A garden plant only—it is rarely found growing wild.

To cultivate: Sow in ground (well-drained, sunny spot) late spring. Allow 1 foot between plants. Goes to seed if not kept watered.

Parts used: leaves and seeds.

Time to pick: leaves throughout the growing season. The seed in autumn, when brown and dry.

Use dill leaves with cucumbers, in soups, and when cooking vegetables such as beans, carrots and cabbage. Add to potato and other vegetable salads and to scrambled eggs. Use leaves and seeds when making pickles or chutneys and summer drinks.

Medicinally, the infusion is good for the digestion. Chew seeds for bad breath.

Elder

SAMBUCUS NIGRA

A large hardy bush or tree, elder can grow up to 30 feet (9m) high. Each leaf is made up of 5 leaflets, finely toothed and smooth. The creamy white flowers grow in flat-topped clusters and appear in June and July. The berries which follow are shiny black on red stalks. It can be found growing wild in hedges, woods and on waste land throughout the country.

To cultivate: propagate by dividing roots or taking cuttings from bare shoots in autumn. Plant in a moist sunny position. Prune established bushes in early spring before growth starts.

Parts used: flowers and berries.

Time to pick: flowers in June and July, berries in September and October when ripe and hanging downwards.

Use elderflowers for teas, summer drinks, wines and ices. Berries should always be used cooked for wines, sauces, jams, jellies and fruit pies. Use dried berries in place of currants in baking.

Medicinally, use elderflowers for a soothing drink and to make an ointment for chilblains and chapped hands.

Garlic

ALLIUM SATIVUM

A hardy perennial of the onion family, garlic grows 1–3 feet (30–90cm) high. It has long flat narrow leaves tapering to a point. The bulb is made up of small bulblets called cloves and these have a strong pungent flavor. The flowers are greenish white and grow on stalks directly from the bulb. A cultivated plant only. The true garlic is unlikely to be found growing wild.

To cultivate: Plant cloves 2 inches deep, 8 inches apart in March or October, in rich soil, full sun. *Cut flowers off.*

Parts used: the bulbs.

Time to pick: Dig up bulbs when leaves have died down in September.

Use dried garlic as seasoning. Use fresh cloves sparingly to bring out the flavors in all savory dishes. Add to mushrooms, soups and salads.

Medicinally, garlic is good for the digestion.

Hawthorn

CRATAEGUS OXYCANTHA

A deciduous bush or tree, hawthorn is very quick growing. Often used as a thorny hedge plant. The leaves are small and shiny and are divided roughly into three lobes. The tiny flowers, which can be white or pink, grow in clusters and appear in May or June. The haws or fruits follow in the autumn and are bright red with a yellowish pulp and 2 or 3 seeds inside. It can be found growing wild in hedges and along roadsides throughout the country.

To cultivate: for hedging, plant young thorn sets from November to March in rich ordinary soil 4 inches (10cm) apart for a single row and 6 inches (15cm) apart for a double row. Plant trees and shrubs in woods and shrubberies. Prune in July and August.

Parts used: flowers, fruit (haws) and seeds.

Time to pick: flowers in May, haws in October when fully ripe and firm, and throughout the winter for the seeds.

Use flowers for a soothing tea, in wines and summer drinks. Use haws for a jelly and seeds as coffee substitute.

Honeysuckle

LONICERA PERICLYMENUM

A fragrant climbing perennial shrub, honeysuckle can grow up to 20 feet (6m) high. The leaves are a thin oval shape and smooth. The creamy-white flowers are stalkless and grow in whorls of three or four trumpet-shaped blossoms at the end of the branches. They appear from June to September. The fruit is a fleshy red berry. It can be found growing wild in woods and along hedgerows almost everywhere.

To cultivate: plant seeds or rooted cuttings from October to April in ordinary soil in a sunny position, preferably by a south or west wall or fence. Top dress with manure in March or April. Prune in February when shoots of previous year's growth should be cut to within 1–3 inches (3–7cm) of base. Plants should be watered freely in dry weather.

Parts used: the flowers.

When to pick: June to September.

Use flowers to make syrup for sweetening fruits and puddings and for preserves.
　　　Use in ointment for sunburn.

Horseradish

COCHLEARIA ARMORACIA

 A very hardy perennial, horseradish grows 2–3 feet (60–90cm) high with large oblong leaves. Small white flowers appear in July. It can be found growing wild on waste land, but it is mainly a garden plant.

To cultivate: plant young shoots in any position in spring, in well worked soil so that the roots can grow long and straight.

Parts used: the roots.

Time to pick: throughout the growing season.

For drying and preserving dig up a sufficient quantity for roots just before flowering.

Use grated horseradish as a condiment, in salad dressings, cold sauces and herb butters.

Medicinally, use externally as a poultice on insect bites or an embrocation for treating chilblains and easing aching limbs.

Horsetail

EQUISETUM ARVENSE

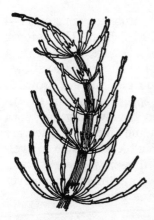

A small herbaceous perennial, horsetail grows 8 inches—2 feet (20–60cm) high. It has frond-like branches and creeping underground rhizomes. In early spring fertile cones grow on erect brown stems. Later, bright green slender-jointed branches appear. It can be found growing abundantly in loam and sandy soils on waste ground.

To cultivate: sow tubers or spores in spring or autumn in a sunny position in a light loam or sandy soil. Once established the plant will quickly spread.

Parts used: green barren stems.

Time to pick: cut the stems close to the base of the plant in June and July.

Medicinally, use a strong infusion of horsetail to restore facial skin tone after illness, and for splitting nails.

Use for cleaning pewter.

Licorice

GLYCYRRHIZA GLABRA

 A perennial shrub, licorice grows 2–4 feet (60–120cm) high. The smooth dark green leaves are divided into 4 or 5 pairs of leaflets. Small yellowy white or purple flowers grow in spikes and appear from June to August. The roots grow very long both downwards and sideways. They are brown and wrinkled outside and yellow inside; they have a sweet taste. Except in warm climates it is never found growing wild.

To cultivate: 6 inch (15cm) lengths of side roots or runners in early spring. Put into well manured rich sandy soil near water but in a very sheltered sunny position. It cannot withstand frost. Plant the lengths 4–6 inches (10–15cm) deep and 18 inches (45cm) apart.

Parts used: the roots.

When to pick: carefully dig up roots in late autumn at the end of the third or fourth season of cultivation. Reserve the soft young shoots for propagation.

Use licorice to sweeten tart stewed fruits and for a thirst-quenching drink.

Medicinally, use the infusion as a gargle for sore throat, and for coughs and chesty colds. It is also a mild laxative. For those who suffer from acne and have a sweet tooth, licorice sweets are the best ones to eat.

Lovage

LEVISTICUM OFFICINALE

A hardy perennial, lovage grows up to 5 feet (150cm) high. The large pale green leaves are divided into leaflets. The greenish yellow flowers grow in large clusters and appear from June to August. It is a cultivated plant only. The wild species, Alexanders, is similar in appearance but with stronger more pungent flavor. It can be found on roadsides and waste land near coasts.

To cultivate: Can be started indoors or out; put in permanent site in autumn or spring, allowing 2 feet between plants. Increase by root division.

Parts used: leaves, stems and seeds.

When to pick: leaves and stems throughout the growing season. Gather seed heads before seeds begin to fall.

Use leaves in broths, sauces and salads, and stems as a vegetable. Use seeds in fruit salad and drinks.

Medicinally, the infusion is good for the digestion and stimulates the kidneys.

Marjoram

ORIGANUM MAJORANA

A perennial plant in warm climates, elsewhere it has to be grown as an annual. It grows about 1 foot (30cm) high with small leaves; the tiny green-white flowers form small bunched heads, which look like knots. They flower in July. Wild marjoram (*origanum vulgare*) can be found growing on chalky soils. It is a perennial and the flowers are pale lilac.

To cultivate: Sow seeds in May in dry, light soil. Thin to 18 inches apart. Divide in spring or autumn, discarding woody centers. Can be grown indoors.

Parts used: the leaves.

Time to pick: throughout the growing season.

Use in soups, salads, sauces, with eggs and cheese and with vegetables.

Medicinally, use a warm infusion for headaches, a hot fomentation for aching limbs and oil of marjoram for toothache.

Mint

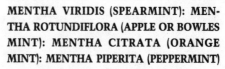

**MENTHA VIRIDIS (SPEARMINT): MEN-
THA ROTUNDIFLORA (APPLE OR BOWLES
MINT): MENTHA CITRATA (ORANGE
MINT): MENTHA PIPERITA (PEPPERMINT)**

All mints are perennials with a creeping, almost galloping rootstock. They
grow 1–2 feet (30–60cm) high and the
flowers, which are varying shades
of pink and purple, appear in late
summer. Spearmint has lance-shaped
leaves and narrow, pointed flower
spikes. Applemint has round woolly
leaves. Orange mint is low-growing
and has smooth dark green leaves
with a purple tinge. Peppermint has
very dark purplish green leaves and
red stalks. Some of the mints can be
found growing wild along the banks
of streams and in other moist soils.

To cultivate: Plant new shoots in spring, or roots in autumn,
10 inches apart. Restrict root growth. Spreads quickly in moist,
rich, partially shaded soil.

Parts used: the leaves.

Time to pick: throughout the growing season.

Use leaves of all mints in drinks, wine and fruit cups, salads
and sauces, with eggs and cheese, in fruit and ices. Add spearmint or Bowles mint to vegetables.

Medicinally, use the infusion as a soothing tea, rub
fresh leaves on the forehead for a headache and use oil of
peppermint for toothache.

Dried mint leaves help to repel moths.

Mugwort

ARTEMISIA VULGARIS

A woody reddish stemmed perennial, mugwort grows 2–3 feet (60–90cm) high. The segmented leaves are dark green, smooth on top and covered with a white down on the underside. The leaf segments are pointed. Small oval-shaped flowers of a pale yellow or reddish tinge appear from July onwards. It can be found growing wild along hedges and roadsides almost everywhere.

To cultivate: propagate by root division or cuttings taken in the spring. Plant 2 feet (60cm) apart in any soil and in any position.

Parts used: leaves and flower shoots.

Time to pick: leaves throughout the growing season, flower buds as they appear.

Use dried flower shoots as seasoning, fresh in raw vegetable salads.

Medicinally, mugwort infusion encourages the appetite. Use for sore and blistered feet.

Use as a moth repellent.

Nasturtium

TROPAEOLUM MAJUS

A hardy climbing or trailing annual, nasturtium has smooth circular leaves. The brilliant orange trumpet-shaped flowers bloom all summer long and are followed by fat seeds. It can sometimes be found growing wild but is mainly a garden plant.

To cultivate: Sow seed April/May; space 12 inches apart. Grows in any soil, good container plant.

Parts used: flowers, leaves and seeds.

When to pick: flowers and leaves throughout summer, seeds in autumn.

Use fresh young leaves and flowers as a last minute addition to green and vegetable salads. Use dried leaves as seasoning. Pickle the seeds to use in place of capers.

Medicinally, use for colds and influenza as it has a high content of vitamin C. Take only in moderation.

Rosehips

ROSA CANINA (DOG OR WILD ROSE)
ROSA RUBIGINOSA (SWEETBRIAR)

The fruit of the perennial wild rose, rosehips are bright scarlet, oval-shaped and appear in autumn. The dog rose grows from 3–9 feet (90cm–2½m) high. The stems are arched and covered with curved thorns. The leaves consist of 3–5 pairs of leaflets. Fragrant pale pink or white flowers appear in June and July. The sweetbriar rose is a smaller shrub. Dog roses can be found growing wild in hedges and fields throughout the country. The sweetbriar is found on chalky soils.

To cultivate: plant bushes 3 feet (90cm) apart in any position in the autumn. Water well until established. Keep in manageable shape by pruning after hips have been gathered.

Parts used: the fruits.

When to pick: after the first frost when the hips will be slightly soft. For drying, pick when firm but fully ripe.

Use fresh or dried hips to make puree, sauces, ices and syrup.
Medicinally, rosehip tea is refreshing and slightly diuretic with a high content of vitamin C.

Rosemary

ROSMARINUS OFFICINALIS

A sweet-scented evergreen shrub, rosemary grows up to 4–5 feet (1–1½m) high in a sheltered position. The spiky leaves are about 1 inch (2½cm) long, green on top and gray beneath. The small pale blue flowers grow in little clusters up the stems. It can be found growing wild only in warm climates.

To cultivate: Set plants in sandy, dry soil in spring. 3 feet of space needed around mature plants; may be cut back. Take stem cuttings, divide roots or layer side shoots in May. Good container plant.

Parts used: leaves.

When to pick: throughout the year.

Use fresh or dried leaves in fruit cups, soups, eggs and vegetables, jellies and vinegars, honey.

Medicinally the leaves make a slightly diuretic tea and a stimulating wine. Use as a moth repellent.

Sage

SALVIA OFFICINALIS

An evergreen woody stemmed shrub, sage grows up to 2 feet (60cm) high. The stalked slender leaves are grayish green and rough textured. The flowers are purplish blue and appear in July. Other varieties of sage differ in color, size of leaf and flavor. Some are purely ornamental. A variety of sage called Clary (*salvia sclarea*) can be found growing wild in dry fields and by roadsides.

To cultivate: Sow seeds in dry sunny position in April/May, thin to 1½ feet apart. After 3–4 years becomes woody and should be divided. Take stem cuttings in May. Suitable container plant.

Parts used: leaves

When to pick: throughout the year.

Use fresh or dried leaves in soups and sauces, in stuffing for fowl, with cheese and vegetables and in fruit cups.

Medicinally the infusion makes a gargle and mouthwash. Make sage tea for sleeplessness and an oil for healing bruises.

Salad Burnet

SANGUISORBA MINOR

A low-growing almost prostrate perennial, salad burnet grows up to 1 foot (30cm) high. The leaves are divided into 6 or 7 pairs of leaflets. The little round flowerheads are a reddish green and appear from June onwards. It can sometimes be found growing wild in chalky soils.

To cultivate: Sow seeds in full sun in April or May; allow 1 foot between rows. Roots may be divided in autumn.

Parts used: the leaves.

When to pick: almost all year round, but the cucumber flavor is stronger in summer months.

Use fresh or dried in soups, salads and sauces, in summer drinks and cups, and vinegars.

Soapwort

SAPONARIA OFFICINALIS

A herbaceous perennial, soapwort grows up to 2 feet (60cm) high, with a stout stem and smooth lance-shaped leaves. The stems creep along the ground and form roots at the nodules. Clusters of large pink flowers appear in August and September. The scent of the flowers becomes more pronounced in the evenings and attracts the hawkmoths. It can be found growing wild on banks and along roadsides. An easy plant to grow in the garden.

To cultivate: sow seed in April in a flowering position in a moist but sunny spot. Take rooted cuttings or divide plants in November and plant 2 feet apart.

Parts used: leaves and roots. Time to pick: leaves throughout the summer, dig up roots in autumn.

Use a decoction of the plant in place of detergent or soap for washing delicate fabrics and for a hair shampoo.

Summer Savory

SATUREIA HORTENSIS

A hardy annual, summer savory grows to 1 foot (30cm) high, with small smooth leaves on slender stems. The tiny flowers are pinky white and appear in July.

To cultivate: Sow seeds in spring after frost in moist rich soil in sun. Thin to 12 inches apart. Suitable for containers.

Winter Savory

SATUREIA MONTANA

A hardy dwarf perennial, winter savory grows 6–12 inches (15–30cm) high. It has woody stems and rather tough little leaves, which have a milder taste than those of summer savory. Neither of the savories are found growing wild.

To cultivate: Same as summer savory but sow in August/September or divide roots in spring.

Parts used: the leaves.

When to pick: summer savory throughout the growing season, winter savory throughout the year.

Use both savories fresh or dried in soups, salads and sauces, eggs and cheese, and with vegetables, especially beans of all kinds.

Medicinally, take savory tea for indigestion.

Sweet Cicely

MYRRHIS ODORATA

A hardy perennial, sweet cicely grows from 2–3 feet (60–90cm) high. It is hollow-stemmed and has large downy fernlike leaves. The white flowers grow in clusters and start blooming in May. It can sometimes be found growing wild in shady places as a garden escape.

To cultivate: Plant seedlings in drained soil in partial shade. Allow 18 inches between mature plants. Self-sows freely. Needs continuous removal of flowers.

Part used: leaves and seeds.

When to pick: leaves throughout the growing season and seeds in late autumn.

Use fresh or dried leaves in salads and with all tart fruits; it acts as a sugar saver. Use in summer drinks. Use leaves or seeds when cooking cabbage and cauliflower.

Medicinally, the tea improves the appetite and digestion.

The leaves and seeds are used in a fragrant polish for furniture and floors.

Thyme

THYMUS VULGARIS (GARDEN THYME)
THYMUS CITRIODORA (LEMON THYME)

A small perennial growing 6–10 inches (15–25cm) high, garden thyme has woody stems, tiny leaves and pale mauve flowers which appear in June. Lemon thyme is a smaller plant but has larger leaves and a distinct lemon smell and flavor. Wild thyme (*thymus serpyllum*) can be found growing on grassy banks on rather dry, light or chalky soils.

To cultivate: Set plants in dry, chalky soil, full sun, 12–18 inches apart. Take cuttings or divide in May. Compact, suitable for containers.

Parts used: the leaves.

When to pick: all year round.

Use fresh or dried in soups and sauces and with cheese, vegetables and in vinegars. Add lemon thyme to fruits and jellies.

Medicinally, use the infusion for sleeplessness, for chesty coughs, for bathing sore eyes and for aching limbs. Use in an ointment for spots and pimples.

Use to repel insects and to act as disinfectant.

Verbascum

VERBASCUM THAPSIFORME
VERBASCUM THAPSUS

A single stemmed biennial, verbascum grows 4–5 feet (120–150cm) high on a flat rosette of large woolly leaves. The bright yellow flowers grow in dense spikes at the top of the stems and appear from June to August. It grows wild almost everywhere and is an easy garden plant.

To cultivate: Sow seed in August, transplant in October. Allow 1½–2 feet between plants. Will grow in most any soil, in sunny sheltered position.

Parts used: the flowers.

Time to pick: on dry days as the flowers appear.

Use fresh (immediately after picking) or dried flowers to make a medicinal infusion for coughs, colds and sleeplessness. Externally, use the oil to heal bruises and ease hemorrhoids.

Woodruff

ASPERULA ODORATA

A perennial with a creeping rootstock, woodruff grows 6–10 inches (15–25cm) high. The leaves grow in whorls or ruffs around slender erect stems, about 6 to 7 to each stem. The tiny white starlike flowers appear in May and June. It is a fairly common wild plant growing in woods and shady places.

To cultivate: propagate by dividing the rootstock in spring. Plant 4 inches apart in a fully shaded position in a light but rich soil. Keep well watered until established.

Parts used: the leaves.

When to pick: April or May just before the flowers appear.

Use fresh, wilted, or dried leaves in summer drinks and in wines and cups made with soft fruit.

Medicinally, use to make a stimulating tea.

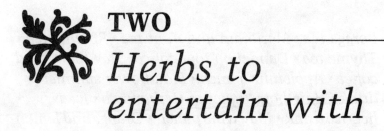

TWO

Herbs to entertain with

Borage tea • Marjoram and mint tea • Rosehip tea • Thyme tea • Dandelion root coffee • Hawthorn seed coffee • Applemint punch • Elderflower summer drink • Hawthorn liqueur • Herb punch • Iced licorice drink • May wine punch • Orange and lemon mint drink • Red wine cup • Rosemary wine • Woodruff wine cup • Apple juice and sage • Carrot juice • Celery juice • Grapefruit juice • Mixed vegetable juice • Tomato juice • Herb seasonings : single herbs • herb mixtures • herb butters • Angelica tea • Dill seed tea • Elderflower tea • Hawthorn tea • Sweet cicely tea • Herbs in flower arrangements

Herbs can be used either fresh or dried in the majority of recipes. When dried herbs are used it should be remembered that they have a more concentrated flavor, so that the measured quantity will be stronger than that of the fresh herb. Where a recipe demands a fresh herb which you cannot find, it is suggested you use half the amount of dried herb. For directions on drying herbs see *Choosing, Planting and Cultivating Herbs* by Philippa Back (Keats, 1977).

Dried herbs have a definite shelf life and their flavors, scents and colors gradually deteriorate. No herb should be kept for longer than 10–12 months.

Refreshing teas

Herb teas are an enjoyable way of taking something that does you good, and the suggestions which follow make a pleasant change from Indian or China tea.

To make tea sufficient for two tea cups: into a warmed pot put 4 teaspoons fresh crushed or finely chopped herb (experiment to find the strength you prefer). Pour on 2 cups of boiling water. Cover and allow to stand 5–6 minutes. Strain and drink hot. Sweeten with honey if desired.

For iced tea, and a stronger flavor, add more herb. Cover the infusion and leave until cold. Chill in the refrigerator or add ice.

Borage Tea

Make in the above manner, adding the flowers as well as the leaves. It has a refreshing cucumber flavor.

Drink occasionally, hot or iced, as a stimulating tea.

Marjoram and mint tea

Follow the general directions for making teas, using 3 parts marjoram leaves to 1 part mint.

Rosehip tea

The tea is made from dried finely chopped rosehips which should be soaked overnight in just enough water to cover them. Next day simmer gently 1 tablespoon rosehips in a covered pan in 1½ pints water for about ½–¾ hour.

Add a pinch of lemon thyme for a delicious lemony flavor. Strain and sweeten with a little honey if desired. Drink hot or cold.

Rosemary tea

Use leaves and/or flowering tops for this stimulating tea, and follow the general directions.

Thyme tea

Use leaves of either garden or lemon thyme and follow the general directions. Add a little sage to garden thyme for extra flavor. Lemon thyme makes a very fragrant tea. Both teas are best served hot.

Coffee substitutes

Dandelion coffee

Dig up dandelion roots, wash and scrub them thoroughly. Spread the roots out on thick brown paper and leave to dry slowly in a warm place. This will take several days, but it is important, as it seals in the flavor. When dry put the roots, roughly chopped, on to a baking tray. Roast in the oven at 350°F for about an hour, or until the pieces are a nice even brown. Be careful they do not become too dark. When ready, remove and grind to a fine powder. Store in a screw-top jar. Use 1 or 2 teaspoons in a cup of boiling water.

Hawthorn seed coffee

Gather haws on a dry day during autumn or winter. Split open the berries with a sharp knife and remove the seeds—there are 2–3 seeds in each berry. Wear rubber gloves for this job as the berries stain the skin badly. Thoroughly wash the seeds. Put on to kitchen foil and fold like a parcel. Place in a moderately hot oven (350°F) for about 1 hour or until a deep even brown. Allow to cool, then grind and use as ordinary coffee.

Herbs in wine, spirits and sparkling drinks

Applemint punch

12 sprigs applemint or 2 large handfuls
juice of 6 oranges
juice of 3 lemons
½ cup raw sugar
3 cups cider
7 cups (1½ liters) ginger ale

Crush the mint and pour over it the orange and lemon juices. Add the sugar and stir well. Put ice into a punch bowl and pour the mixture over it. Add the cider and ginger ale.

A delicious and refreshing drink-herb punch made with borage, spearmint and marigold petals.

Elderflower summer drink
2 *large lemons*
2 *lbs. raw sugar*
2 *tablespoons citric acid*
15–20 *flower heads*
4 *cups boiling water*

Slice the lemons and put into a bowl with the sugar, citric acid and the flower heads. Pour over boiling water and cover. Leave for about 2 days. Strain through a cloth. Pour into bottles and seal. Store in a cool place. Use to flavor fruit cups, fruit salads and ices. It makes a refreshing long drink when diluted with soda water.

Hawthorn liqueur
hawthorn blossom
brandy

Fill a clean dry jar three-quarters full of freshly gathered hawthorn blossom. Fill the jar to the top with brandy and cork tightly. Stand in a cool place for about 3 months or longer if the flavor is not sufficiently developed. Strain and bottle. Drink as a digestive or use for flavoring custards or fruit salads.

Herb punch
6 *cups boiling water*
1 *large handful spearmint*
2 *large handfuls borage*
juice of 6 lemons
juice of 2 oranges
1 *cup pineapple juice*
5 *cups strong tea*
1 *cup corn syrup*
4 *quarts ginger ale*
bunch of fresh washed mint
calendula petals

Pour 6 cups boiling water over the mint leaves and allow to steep for 20 minutes. Strain and pour into a large bowl over the borage, fruit juices, tea and syrup. Leave overnight. Strain over ice and add ginger ale, fresh mint leaves and calendula petals.

Iced licorice drink

Dissolve a 2-inch stick of licorice (available at health food stores) in 2 cups boiling water. Cool and keep in the refrigerator.

To serve: half fill a glass with the licorice drink and top up with soda water. Add a sprig of peppermint and a lump of ice for a thirst-quenching drink.

May wine punch

bunch of woodruff (wilted)
1 tablespoon fresh chopped sweet cicely
1 bottle dry white wine
1 tablespoon sugar
cherries or strawberries
grated rind and juice of an orange
¼ cup Cointreau or other liqueur
4 cups (32 ounces) club soda

Put woodruff and sweet cicely in a wide-mouthed jar. Pour on a third of the white wine. Cover the jar and leave for 6–8 hours. Dissolve sugar in a little boiling water and leave to cool. Wash fruit and place in a bowl. Add rind and juice of the orange to the wine and herbs, then strain on to the fruit together with the remaining wine, sugar syrup, liqueur and soda. Serve well chilled.

Orange and lemon mint drink

rind and juice of 1 orange
rind and juice of ½ lemon

1 teaspoon honey
1 teaspoon fresh chopped mint leaves
1¼ cup boiling water

Wash the fruit and peel the rinds thinly. Put rinds, honey and mint leaves in a jug. Add boiling water. Cover and leave until cold. Add orange and lemon juices. Strain and dilute with club soda to taste.

Red wine cup

⅓ cup raw sugar
1 bottle red wine
grated rind of 1 orange
½ cup brandy
3 or 4 sprigs lemon thyme
handful of fresh borage leaves
salad burnet leaves
4 cups (32 ounces) club soda

Dissolve sugar in a little boiling water and leave to cool. Into a jug put the red wine, orange rind, brandy, lemon thyme and borage leaves. Sweeten to taste with the sugar syrup. Stand the jug in the refrigerator for one hour. Strain, add soda and ice cubes and garnish with salad burnet leaves.

Rosemary wine

6 fresh rosemary sprigs
2 cups white wine

Gather the rosemary in the morning; wash the sprigs only if absolutely necessary. Place them in a jug and pour over the wine. Cover and leave for 2–3 days. Strain the wine and chill lightly before serving.

Woodruff wine cup
bunch of fresh woodruff (pick and leave until wilted)
1 bottle of light white wine
juice of ½ an orange or lemon
fresh fruit—peaches or wild strawberries
club soda

Put woodruff into a bowl and add wine to cover. Infuse for about an hour. Strain and add the orange or lemon juice. Add the fresh fruit and lastly the remaining wine. Chill lightly. Just before serving, add soda to taste.

 Fruit and vegetable juices

Fresh juices make an appetizing and healthy start to a meal. The ideal way of making them is to use an electric juice extractor. A blender can be used, though with hard fruits or root vegetables a little liquid should be added—either water or stock—to avoid too heavy a load on the motor.

To prepare: wash fruit or vegetable and scrape or peel where necessary. Remove pits from fruit, cut up herbs and chop fruit or vegetable into small pieces before putting through juice extractor.

Where no mechanical aid is available, fruit and vegetables can be cut up or grated by hand onto a piece of muslin, the herbs added and the juice squeezed out by twisting the muslin hard.

All home-made juices should be drunk as soon as possible after making as they quickly lose their color, flavor and health-giving properties.

For quick and easy fruit and vegetables juices, buy them in bottles. Mix with the herbs and seasonings of your choice and allow to stand for ½ hour. Serve chilled.

Apple juice and sage

Prepare enough apples to yield 1 cup juice; this will depend on the size and texture of the apples. Add 1 teaspoon fresh chopped sage. Extract juice and sweeten to taste. This is one generous serving.
Alternatively stir the sage into a bottle of apple juice.

Carrot juice

Prepare enough carrots to yield 1 cup juice. Add ½ teaspoon each fresh chopped marjoram and salad burnet. Season to taste and serve in glasses which have been rubbed over with a cut clove of garlic. Makes 2 small glasses. Serve at once.

Celery juice

Prepare enough celery to yield 2 cups juice. Add 1 teaspoon each fresh chopped lovage, parsley and chives. Extract juice, season to taste and add 1 teaspoon lemon juice and a little light cream for a really smooth drink. Makes 4 small glasses.

Grapefruit juice

Squeeze enough ripe grapefruit to yield 1 cup juice, using a lemon squeezer. Add 1 teaspoon lemon juice, 1 teaspoon honey and ½ teaspoon each fresh chopped angelica and sweet cicely.

Mixed vegetable juice

Prepare a sufficient number of carrots, tomatoes and spinach leaves to yield 2 cups juice—use in proportion 2 parts carrot, 2 parts tomatoes and 1 part spinach. Add 1 teaspoon sweet cicely and ½ teaspoon each fresh chopped chives and parsley. Extract juice, season to taste and serve at once. Makes 4 glasses.
If using canned juice, add a pinch of basil to the above herbs. Chill and serve.

Tomato juice
juice of ½ lemon
salt and pepper
1 teaspoon honey sugar
3 teaspoons fresh chopped basil
2 cups tomato juice

Mix all the ingredients together well and chill in the refrigerator for at least 1 hour before serving.

 ## Herb seasonings

Use all herb seasonings with a fair amount of caution so that they bring out the natural flavors of food rather than overpower them. The herb is dried and then ground in a mortar or minced sufficiently finely for it to be kept in a salt cellar.

The strong herbs are naturally the ones to be used singly, while herb mixtures can include the mild flavors. The strong herbs retain their flavor and aroma for a longer period, but even these will be of little use after a month or so. When not on the table they should be kept in a cool dark cupboard.

Single herbs to add sparingly to soups and stews, meat and fish:

> basil, lovage, rosemary,
> dill, marjoram, summer savory,
> garlic, peppermint, thyme

To sweet dishes add lemon thyme, angelica and sweet cicely.

The more fragrant herbs come into their own in the mixtures. An attractive bowl of freshly gathered herbs lends an appetizing smell to the table and a flavor to green salads and salad dressings.

Unless dried herbs are reconstituted in a little lemon juice they are not really suitable for salads.

Suggested herb mixtures, dried or fresh:

1. *1 part lovage*
   2 parts parsley
   1 part savory

2. *1 part dandelion*
   1 part dill
   2 parts borage

3. *1 part marigold or calendula*
   1 part mint
   2 parts salad burnet

4. *1 part rosemary*
   1 part mugwort
   2 parts parsley

Suggested sweet herb mixtures:

1. *1 part angelica*
   2 parts sweet cicely
   1 part mint

2. *1 part lemon thyme*
   1 part honeysuckle
   2 parts sweet cicely

When making your own mixtures the following parts should be remembered:

1. Avoid using all strong herbs together—the conflicting flavors will spoil the end result.

2. Similarly, do not use only mild-flavored herbs.

3. If you grow your own herbs, decide which are your strong and which your mild herbs. Remember that their strength can vary at different times of the year.

4. Mix herbs together in the proportion of ⅓ strong and ⅔ mild. You can follow this principle throughout whether you use one, three or five herbs in the mixture.

Herb butters

A herb butter is not a seasoning in the true sense, but it is an attractive way to add relish to food at the table and is especially nice for canapes and delicate tea sandwiches. Fresh or dried herbs can be used. Add herbs to butter in the proportion 2–3 tablespoons fresh chopped herbs to ¼ lb. slightly salted butter and 1 teaspoon lemon juice. Soften the butter, add the herbs and blend well together. For dried herbs use 2–3 teaspoons of herb to the same quantity of butter, and add a little extra lemon juice. This gives piquancy and helps to reconstitute the herb, extracting its full flavor. Make up the herb butter several hours before required and chill in refrigerator, where it will keep for a number of days.

Flavors which are especially good are: basil, dill, crushed dill seed, crushed clove of garlic, grated horseradish root, any of the mints, rosemary, summer savory and the thymes.

You can blend your own mixture using some of the milder herbs as well, such as parsley, chives and marigold.

Use your butter directly on top of grilled meats, hot vegetables or baked potatoes. Use in sandwiches and on crackers. Best of all, use on hot bread rolls or slice a loaf of French bread lengthways, spread each cut side with herb butter, wrap the loaf in tin foil and bake it in a hot oven for 10 minutes.

Soothing teas

To calm the nerves and produce a feeling of relaxation these teas are mild sedatives and digestives.

Angelica tea

Make tea of leaves or stalks following general directions on p. 123. Drink the tea hot immediately after the evening meal as a mild digestive. Sweeten with honey if desired.

Dill seed tea

Pour 1 cup boiling water over 2 teaspoons crushed dill seed and simmer gently for 10 minutes. Strain, reheat and take it hot for a really soothing drink last thing at night.

Elderflower tea

Use dried or fresh flower heads lightly washed. Pour 2 cups boiling water over a large handful of flowers. Cover and allow to stand for 5–10 minutes. Strain. Sweeten with honey if desired. Take hot for an effective sleep-inducing tea last thing at night.

Hawthorn tea

Pour ½ cup boiling water over 1 tablespoon fresh undamaged flowers. Cover and steep for 5–6 minutes. Strain, then sweeten if desired, and drink hot.

Sweet cicely tea

Follow the general directions for making teas on p. 123. This sweet-tasting tea can be made quite strong and needs no added sugar. A good digestive drink when taken hot.

Other soothing teas are savory and peppermint.

 Herbs in flower arrangements

Herb plants can provide material for beautiful flower arrangements, whether you like a huge display of flowers, a small dainty posy or just a simple bouquet. Among the plants there is a wide variety of textured foliage in all shades of green and gray. There are flowers of every color to brighten up the vase and lend freshness to each room.

You may arrange your flowers with infinite care or place them haphazardly into a vase, but certainly you will enjoy to the full the lovely scents and aromas which come from the plants. These are always such a joy to a blind person.

To get full benefit from your flower arrangement, the following points are important:

1. Gather the flower and leaves in the evening after the sun has gone down.

2. Stems which give off a milky fluid when picked should have their ends burnt over a candle for 10 seconds.

3. Plunge them into a sink or bucket full of cold water to come well up the stems. Leave to soak overnight.

4. If you have to shorten a stem for the arrangement, remember to burn the end again.

The following list may help you choose your material for floral arrangements:

Foliage plants
Barberry, lovage, marjoram, mints, mugwort, nasturtium, rosemary, sages, savories and the thymes

Flowers
Angelica, basil, dill, honeysuckle, marigold, marjoram, mugwort, nasturtium, the sages, salad burnet, the savories, sweet cicely, the thymes, verbascum and woodruff

Dried or fresh seed heads offer an unusual display
Angelica, dill, lovage, rosehips, sweet cicely

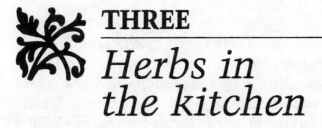

THREE

Herbs in the kitchen

Dill summer soup • Five herb broth • Leek broth • Lovage broth • Marigold chicken broth • Marjoram bean soup • Mint soup • Sage soup • Savory soup • Thyme soup • Broad bean salad • Horseradish cole slaw • Nasturtium salad • Sweet corn salad • Winter salad • Dill herb dressing for salads • Green sauce • Herb cream sauce • Herb mayonnaise • Vinaigrette dressing • Egg dip • Egg mayonnaise • Egg mousse • Lovage soufflé • Sweet herb pancakes • Cheese and potato cakes • Cheese and tomato toast • Cheese pudding • Herb cheese • Mushrooms with cheese • Baked zucchini • Braised leeks • Carrots and dill • Creamed cabbage • Savory lentil • Banana and orange salad • Quince creams • Raspberry charlotte • Strawberry fruit salad • Sweet apples in wine • Applemint ice cream • Gooseberry ice cream • Peppermint sherbet • Thyme sherbet

To cook with herbs is perhaps the most accepted way of using them. You automatically assume that the proper place for herbs is in the kitchen, but few realize how much they contribute to the daily diet.

Herbs greatly improve the flavor of food as well as making it more nourishing. They are full of nutritious substances, one of which, volatile oil, provides each herb with its distinctive flavor and aroma.

Meals become easier to digest, for when herbs are used in cooking their aromas are released. These act upon the olfactory nerves making the digestive juices in the mouth and stomach flow. Thus, when the food is eaten its full value is obtained by the body.

Soups and broths

Dill summer soup
1 cup chicken stock
1 cup tomato juice
½ crushed clove of garlic
3 tablespoons dill
½ cup light cream
½ cup milk
salt and pepper
½ cucumber, finely diced

Mix together the stock, tomato juice, garlic, dill, cream, milk and seasoning. Blend well, then add the cucumber. For a really smooth soup put all the ingredients into the blender and turn on to medium speed for 2 or 3 minutes. Serve well chilled. Serves 4.

Five herb broth

2 *tablespoons oil*
2 *teaspoons each chopped lovage, mint, rosemary, winter savory and parsley*
2 *medium onions, chopped*
1 *tablespoon unbleached flour*
3 *cups stock*
salt and pepper

Heat oil in a pan. Gently sauté the herbs and onions for 2–3 minutes, then add the flour. Cook a further 2 minutes, add stock and seasoning and bring to the boil. Simmer gently for 20–25 minutes. Serves 4.

Leek broth

3 *tablespoons sunflower oil*
2 *leeks, finely chopped*
1 *medium-sized potato, finely sliced*
1 *small clove garlic, finely chopped*
3 *cups stock*
½ *teaspoon caraway seed*
1 *teaspoon each lovage and mint, finely chopped*
seasoning

Heat oil over a low flame. Put in leeks and potato and sauté gently for a few minutes. Add garlic and stir well. Pour in the stock and add caraway seed, lovage and mint. Cover and simmer for 25 minutes or until vegetables are soft. Adjust seasoning. Serves 4.

Lovage broth
4 cups well-flavored brown stock
seasoning
5 tablespoons fresh or dried chopped lovage leaves

Remove all fat from the stock and strain it into pan. Bring to the boil and season to taste. Add the lovage and simmer gently for 10–15 minutes. Serves 4.

Marigold chicken broth
3 tablespoons rice
2 cups strong chicken stock
2 tablespoons dried calendula or marigold petals
salt and pepper

Wash the rice and put in a pan with other ingredients. Bring slowly to the boil and simmer gently until the rice is cooked. Adjust seasoning and serve. Serves 2.

Marjoram bean soup
½ cup butter beans
2–3 tablespoons sunflower oil
2 medium onions, sliced
2 tablespoons fresh chopped marjoram
6 cups stock
salt and pepper

Soak beans overnight. Cook the beans in their soaking water until soft, then drain. Heat oil in a pan over low heat, add onions and cook for 2–3 minutes. Add the marjoram and cook for a further 2 minutes. Add beans, stock and seasoning, bring to the boil, simmer gently for 20–30 minutes. Pass the soup through a sieve or put into a liquidizer. Adjust seasoning, reheat and serve. Serves 6.

Mint soup

2–3 tablespoons sunflower oil
3 medium-sized potatoes
3 tablespoons fresh chopped mint
6 cups stock
salt and pepper

Heat oil in a pan. Add the potatoes, roughly chopped, and the mint. Sauté gently for 3–5 minutes. Pour on the stock and add seasoning. Bring to the boil and simmer until the potatoes are soft—about 20 minutes. Pass the soup through a sieve or put into a liquidizer. Adjust seasoning, reheat and serve. Serves 6.

Sage soup

1 cup red lentils
3 tablespoons sunflower oil
1 medium onion, chopped
1 small clove garlic, chopped
3 tablespoons fresh chopped sage leaves
2 tablespoons tomato puree
4 cups chicken stock
salt and pepper

Wash, cook and drain the lentils. Heat oil in a pan, add onion and garlic. Cook gently for 2–3 minutes. Add the sage and cook a further 2 minutes. Add lentils, tomato puree, stock and seasoning. Cover the pan and simmer for 20–30 minutes, stirring occasionally. Pass the soup through a sieve or put into a liquidizer. Adjust seasoning, reheat and serve. Serves 4–5.

Savory soup

½ cup green split peas
4 cups ham stock
1 onion, sliced

pinch of raw sugar
pepper ·
3 tablespoons fresh summer savory

Soak the peas overnight in some of the stock. Add onion, sugar, pepper, summer savory and the remaining stock. Simmer gently until the peas are soft. Remove from the heat and put through a sieve or into a liquidizer. Adjust seasoning, reheat and serve. Serves 4.

Thyme soup
2–3 tablespoons sunflower oil
1 onion, sliced
4 tablespoons fresh chopped thyme
3 tablespoons unbleached flour
4 cups chicken stock
salt and pepper

Heat oil in a pan. Sauté the onion gently and add the thyme. Finally stir in the flour and allow to cook for a further 2 minutes. Add the stock and seasoning, cover and simmer gently for 20 minutes. Remove from the heat, pass the soup through a sieve or put into a liquidizer. Adjust seasoning, reheat and serve. Serves 4.

 Salads and sauces

Broad bean salad
1 pound young broad beans
1 teaspoon each fresh chopped summer savory and parsley
1 or 2 spring onions
¼ cup cream
2 teaspoons lemon juice
salt and pepper

Cook the beans until tender in boiling salted water to which is added ½ teaspoon summer savory. Drain and cool. Slice the spring onions very thinly and add to the beans. Mix together the cream, lemon juice, remaining herbs and seasoning. Pour the dressing over the beans. Serves 4.

Horseradish cole slaw

2 cups shredded cabbage
2 tablespoons chopped raw onion
2 teaspoons grated fresh horseradish
2 tablespoons mayonnaise
2 tablespoons grated carrot

Mix all the ingredients and serve. Serves 4.

Nasturtium salad

young nasturtium leaves
lettuce
raw carrot
spring onions
a few nasturtium flowers

Using 2 lettuce leaves to every nasturtium leaf, wash them well in salted water, shake off excess moisture and arrange in a dish. Grate carrot on top and sprinkle finely chopped spring onions over the carrot. Garnish with 1 or 2 nasturtium flowers and serve at once.

Add your own mixture of fresh herbs at the table in an oil and lemon dressing. Or serve a cream dressing made by mixing together 4 tablespoons cream, 1 teaspoon lemon juice and ½ teaspoon parsley.

Sweet corn salad

1 cup cooked sweet corn
2 tablespoons each fresh chopped sweet cicely, mint
*   and chives*

1 cup sour cream
2 tomatoes, peeled and chopped
salt and pepper
paprika

In a bowl mix together the sweet corn, herbs, tomato and seasoning. Fold the cream into the mixture. Serve on lettuce sprinkled with paprika. Serves 4.

Winter salad
1 tablespoon dried mugwort
lemon juice
2 cups raw grated Brussels sprouts
½ cup raw grated carrot
½ cup raw grated Jerusalem artichoke
½ cup raw grated beet
3 tablespoons finely chopped onion
2 tablespoons fresh chopped salad burnet
1 tablespoon fresh chopped marjoram

Reconstitute the dried mugwort in a little lemon juice. Arrange the Brussels sprouts on a dish. Mix the carrot, artichoke, beet, onion and herbs together and place on top of the sprouts. Serve with oil and lemon or mayonnaise dressing. Serves 4–6.

Dill herb dressing for salads
½ cup yogurt
½ cup light cream
½ clove garlic, finely chopped
1 teaspoon raw sugar
2 tablespoons parsley
3 tablespoons dill
salt and pepper

Beat the yogurt and cream together until smooth. Add all the other ingredients and blend well. Yield: about 1 cup

Green sauce

2 *tablespoons salad burnet vinegar, see p. 167*
2 *tablespoons white wine*
1 *small onion, finely chopped*
1 *cup well-flavored white sauce*
1 *teaspoon each fresh chopped parsley, lovage and salad burnet*
salt and pepper

Heat the vinegar and wine in a pan and add the chopped onion. Cook until the onion is soft and the liquid reduced by half. Add the white sauce, herbs and seasoning. Bring to a boil and simmer gently for 3–4 minutes. Serve hot with egg, cheese and vegetable dishes. Yield: about 1 cup.

Herb cream sauce

½ *cup sour cream*
1 *teaspoon each fresh chopped parsley and chives*
½ *teaspoon each fresh chopped mint and thyme*
small piece of crushed garlic
salt and pepper

Blend all the ingredients together to make a smooth mixture.
Serve poured over beet salad or hot vegetables such as new potatoes, carrots and spinach. Yield: ½ cup.

Herb mayonnaise

2 *egg yolks*
salt and pepper
1 *cup sunflower oil*
1 *tablespoon lemon juice*
2 *tablespoons mixed fresh chopped mint, chives, parsley and dill*

With a wooden spoon cream the egg yolks with a pinch of salt and pepper until thick. Add oil 2 or 3 drops at a time, stirring well all the time. If the mayonnaise becomes too thick before all the oil is used, add lemon juice or a few drops of hot water. Lastly add the herbs.

Leave for at least half an hour to allow the flavors to blend. Yield: about 1 cup.

Vinaigrette dressing
¼ cup herb vinegar
1 teaspoon French mustard
1 teaspoon honey
a little crushed garlic (optional)
salt and black pepper
¾ cup sunflower oil
1 teaspoon each calendula (or marigold) petals, borage and dill

Mix together the vinegar, mustard, honey, garlic and seasonings. Pour the mixture slowly into the oil, whisking all the time until thick. Lastly add the herbs and stand on one side to allow flavors to blend. Yield: about 1 cup.

 Eggs and cheese

Egg dip
Peel some hard-boiled eggs and mash them well. Add sunflower oil, a dash of Worcestershire, a little prepared mustard, and crushed garlic. Beat all together until smooth. Stir in a mixture of herbs, dill, mint, parsley and calendula or marigold petals. Frequent tasting is required!

Egg mayonnaise
1 egg per person
cucumber
fresh chopped dill
herb mayonnaise, see p. 146

Poach the required number of eggs. Wash and thinly slice the cucumber, use to cover the bottom of individual scallop shells. Sprinkle a little dill over the cucumber and place a poached egg on top. Cover each with a liberal coating off herb mayonnaise. Garnish with mint leaves. Serve cold.

Egg mousse
4 hard-boiled eggs
½ cup mayonnaise
3 teaspoons gelatin
¼ cup water
½ teaspoon anchovy paste
2 tablespoons mixed fresh chopped mint, parsley, thyme and chives—or your own mixture
pinch black pepper
¼ cup cream

Mash the eggs with a fork and mix with the mayonnaise. Dissolve the gelatin in water and add the anchovy paste. Stir into the egg mixture with the herbs and seasoning. Lightly whip the cream and fold into the eggs. Turn into a mold and leave to set. Turn out on to a bed of lettuce and garnish with tomato and a pinch of basil. Serves 3–4.

Lovage soufflé
4 tablespoons butter
4 tablespoons unbleached flour
1 cup milk
2 teaspoons fresh chopped chives
4 eggs separated
¼ pound mild hard cheese, grated
salt and pepper
4 tablespoons fresh chopped lovage
1–2 tablespoons breadcrumbs
Preheat oven to 375°F.

A summer spread including lovage soufflé, sweet herb pancakes, marjoram bean soup and applemint ice cream.

Melt the butter in a pan and stir in the flour. Add milk and chives and stir until boiling. Boil until thick. Cool slightly and beat in the egg yolks one at a time. Add the cheese, seasoning and lovage and mix well. Whisk the egg whites until firm and fold them into the mixture. Pour carefully into a buttered soufflé dish and sprinkle with breadcrumbs. Bake in a fairly hot oven until well risen and firm to the touch. Serves 4.

Sweet herb pancakes

1 cup unbleached or wholegrain flour
pinch of salt
1 egg
1 cup milk
1 tablespoon melted butter
1 tablespoon hawthorn liqueur, see p. 127
1 teaspoon each fresh chopped sweet cicely and angelica

Make a smooth batter with the flour, salt, egg and milk. Beat well and add melted butter, liqueur and herbs. Leave for ½ hour. Use a small frying pan and about 2 tablespoons batter for each pancake. Brown them on both sides. Roll up the pancakes and serve plain with orange slices and sugar, or fill with fruit.

Cheese and potato cakes

4 cooked potatoes
1 cup grated cheese
1 teaspoon each fresh chopped mint and marjoram
salt and pepper
2 egg yolks

Mash the potatoes and mix with the cheese, herbs and seasoning. Bind the mixture with the egg yolks and shape into flat cakes. Roll each in a little flour and fry in butter or oil until golden brown. Serves 4.

Cheese and tomato toast

1 cup grated cheddar cheese
½ teaspoon French mustard
pinch of paprika
2 tablespoons breadcrumbs
1 teaspoon fresh chopped basil
1 teaspoon fresh chopped summer savory
¾ cup tomato puree
salt and pepper

Put cheese, mustard, paprika and breadcrumbs into a pan. Mix the herbs with the tomato puree and add to the cheese mixture. Stir over a low heat until the mixture is smooth—don't let it boil. Add seasoning and serve on slices of hot toast. Serves 4.

Cheese pudding

2 tablespoons butter
¾ cup breadcrumbs
1 cup milk
1 cup grated hard cheese
2 eggs
2 tablespoons fresh chopped sage
salt and pepper
Preheat oven to 400°F.

Put the butter and breadcrumbs into a bowl. Boil up the milk and pour over the breadcrumbs. Add the cheese—reserving a little for the top—the yolks of eggs, sage and seasoning. Mix well. Whisk the egg whites until stiff and fold them into the mixture. Pour it into a greased pie dish, sprinkle cheese on top and bake in a fairly hot oven until brown. Serves 3–4.

Herb cheese

½ pound cheddar cheese

2 tablespoons mixed fresh chopped thyme, summer savory, parsley and lovage

2 tablespoons heavy cream

2 tablespoons sherry

Grate the cheese or mash well with a fork. Add the herbs and cream, blending well. Lastly add the sherry. Allow the cheese to blend with other flavors before serving.

Mushrooms with cheese

Preheat oven to 350°F.

Wash and peel 1 or 2 large flat mushrooms per person. Remove the stalks, chop them finely and add freshly made breadcrumbs and a generous amount of mixed herbs—parsley, summer savory, tarragon and mint. Add a little crushed garlic, grated cheese and seasoning. Bind the mixture with egg and place on top of the mushrooms. Put the mushrooms in individual dishes and cover each with cheese sauce. Sprinkle with cheese and breadcrumbs. Bake for 20–30 minutes.

 Vegetables

Sautéed zucchini

1 pound zucchini

4 tablespoons butter

2 teaspoons fresh chopped thyme

salt and pepper

Wash, wipe and slice the zucchini thinly. Melt the butter in a pan, add the zucchini, thyme and seasoning. Cover and cook over a low heat until tender. Serves 4.

Braised leeks

Choose young, evenly sized leeks and wash them well. Butter a shallow casserole liberally and sprinkle in 1 tablespoon of mixed fresh chopped herbs—thyme, marjoram and chives. Lay the leeks on top and add enough milk or stock to cover the bottom of the dish. Cover and cook very slowly until leeks are tender.

Carrots and dill
Preheat oven to 350°F.

Prepare the carrots and leave them whole. Put into a buttered casserole. Pour on sufficient liquid made up of half water and half dill vinegar, see p. 167. Add seasoning, ½ teaspoon fresh chopped basil, ½ tablespoon dill, ½ tablespoon sugar and a knob of butter. Cover and cook in a moderate oven until the carrots are tender.

Creamed cabbage

Wash a cabbage and shred it coarsely. Peel and slice one small onion. Put a little cold water in a pan with the onion, a pinch of salt and 2 tablespoons fresh chopped sweet cicely. Bring to the boil and add the cabbage.

In another pan melt 2 tablespoons butter, stir in 2 tablespoons unbleached flour and cook gently. Add a little of the cabbage water to make a thick sauce, and season to taste. Strain the cabbage and, over a gentle heat, add the sauce, stirring well until smooth and well mixed. Serve piping hot.

Savory lentils
1 pound red lentils
2 cups cooked mashed potatoes
1 onion, finely chopped
2 teaspoons fresh chopped rosemary
salt and pepper

Wash the lentils and put into a pan with enough water to cover. Bring to the boil and simmer gently until the lentils are soft and all the liquid taken up. Towards end of cooking, preheat oven to 350°F. Be careful not to let them burn. Mix the lentils, potatoes, onion and herb together. Season to taste. Put all into a greased pie dish and bake in a moderately hot oven until brown on top—about 45 minutes. Serves 4.

 Fruit and ices

Banana and orange salad

½ cup raw sugar
½ cup water
2 teaspoons fresh chopped peppermint
3 bananas
3 oranges

Make up the syrup by boiling sugar, water and peppermint together for 10 minutes. Allow to cool. Prepare fruit and put into a glass bowl. Strain cooled syrup over the top and decorate with fresh chopped peppermint leaves. Serves 4.

Quince creams

½ cup quince jelly
3 tablespoons water
2 tablespoons fresh chopped applemint
½ cup heavy cream, whipped
cochineal (optional)

Put jelly water and applemint into a pan and bring slowly to the boil, stirring often. Simmer gently for 2–3 minutes. Remove from the heat and leave covered overnight, to allow applemint to permeate. Put the mixture into a blender, then through a sieve into a bowl. Fold in the stiffly whipped cream and add a drop or two of cochineal to color it a delicate shade of pink. Spoon into individual glasses and decorate with pep-permint flakes, see p. 169.

Raspberry charlotte

1½ cups breadcrumbs
5 tablespoons raw sugar
3 tablespoons fresh chopped sweet cicely
1 teaspoon fresh chopped lemon thyme
1 pound raspberries
Preheat oven to 400°F.

Mix the breadcrumbs, sugar and herbs together. Butter a pie dish, cover the bottom with the breadcrumb mixture and put a layer of fruit on top. Repeat the layers until the dish is full, finishing with the crumbs. Dot with butter and bake for about 30 minutes. Serves 3–4.

Strawberry fruit salad

1 pound strawberries
1–2 tablespoons raw sugar
¼ cup light cream
¼ cup plain yogurt
3 tablespoons fresh chopped sweet cicely
1 teaspoon fresh chopped angelica

Put the strawberries in a dish and sprinkle on the sugar. Mix together until smooth the cream, yogurt and herbs. Add to the strawberries and mix well. Leave for ½ hour to allow flavors to blend. Serve chilled. Serves 3–4.

Sweet apples in wine

Preheat oven to 275°F.

Peel, core and cut up apples into very thin slices. Butter a deep dish and put in a layer of apple. Sprinkle with a mixture of sugar, angelica stalks finely chopped, and a pinch of lemon thyme. Repeat the layers until the dish is full. Pour over about ½ cup white wine. Cover well and cook in a slow oven for about 4 hours. Leave to cool. When cold, whip up with a fork and pour into a glass dish. Serve chilled with thin cream.

Applemint ice cream
½ cup heavy cream
½ cup raw sugar
1 egg
3 teaspoons lemon juice
4 tablespoons fresh chopped applemint
pinch of salt
1 cup milk

Beat together cream, sugar and egg until thick. Stir in the lemon juice, mint and salt. Add the milk and blend well. Turn mixture into a shallow container. Freeze until it is just firm—about 1 hour. Whisk the ice cream again thoroughly. Return it to the freezer and leave for 4 hours. Serve garnished with fresh or candied mint leaves. Serves 4.

Gooseberry ice cream
¾ pound gooseberries
2 tablespoons fresh chopped angelica stem
2 tablespoons fresh chopped sweet cicely
2 tablespoons sugar
1 cup light cream
green coloring (optional)

Top, tail and wash the gooseberries. Put into a pan with the angelica, sweet cicely and the sugar. Simmer gently until the gooseberries are very soft. Rub the fruit through a sieve and, when cold, stir in the cream. Add a few drops of green coloring to make it a delicate shade of green if desired. Freeze until firm. Decorate with candied angelica. Serves 4.

Peppermint sherbet

1 cup raw sugar
2 cups water
juice and rind of ½ lemon
1 cup fresh chopped peppermint leaves
1 egg white

Put the sugar, water and lemon rind into a pan and bring to the boil. Boil for 5 minutes. Remove from the heat and immediately add the peppermint leaves. Cover and leave until cold. Add the lemon juice and strain. Place in the freezer for about 1 hour. Beat egg white to a stiff froth and whisk it into the water ice. Return ice to the freezer and freeze until firm. Serves 4–6.

Thyme sherbet

1 cup raw sugar
2 cups water
rind of 1 lemon
rind of 2 oranges
3 tablespoons chopped thyme
1 cup freshly squeezed orange juice
juice of 1 lemon

Put sugar, water and lemon rind into a pan and bring to the boil. Boil for 5 minutes. Pare orange rind thinly into a bowl and add the thyme. Pour the boiling syrup on top. Cover and leave until cold. Add orange and lemon juice. Strain and freeze. Serves 6–8.

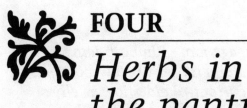

FOUR

Herbs in the pantry

Apple jam • Greengage jam • Rhubarb jam •
Rosemary honey • Barberry jelly • Hawthorn jelly •
Sage jelly • White currant & elderflower jelly •
Apple chutney • Beet relish • Cucumber chutney •
Green tomato chutney • Pickled nasturtium seeds •
Tomsitina • Herb vinegars • Elderflower vinegar •
garlic vinegar • Gooseberry preserve • Honeysuckle
conserves • Peppermint flakes • Rosehip syrup

Herbs in the pantry takes you to the shelves where herbs can provide some unusual and delightful flavors—inexpensive and fun to try out. You can always experiment with your own combination of herb and fruit, or herb and vegetable, once you recognize the individual flavors of the various herbs.

Jams and jellies

Apple jam
3 pounds apples
grated rind and juice of 1 lemon
1 teaspoon ground ginger
2 cups water
2 lbs. raw sugar
⅓ cup crystallized ginger
3 tablespoons fresh chopped sweet cicely
1 tablespoon calendula or marigold petals

Wash, peel, core and cut up the apples. Put the peel and cores in cheesecloth and hang in the pan. Put in the apples, lemon juice and rind, ground ginger and water. Cook until soft. Remove the bag of peel. Add sugar, cystallized ginger (chopped small) and sweet cicely. Stir until the sugar is dissolved. Boil quickly until setting point is reached, about 10 minutes. Five minutes before the end, add the marigold petals. Pour the jam into warmed jars and seal the tops. Yield: 4–5 lbs.

Greengage jam

2 *pounds greengages*
1 *cup water*
3 *tablespoons fresh chopped thyme*
juice of 1 lemon
1½ *lbs. raw sugar*

Wipe the fruit, cut in half and remove the pits. Put into a pan with water, herb and lemon juice. Bring to the boil. Add sugar and stir until dissolved. Bring quickly to the boil and boil rapidly until setting point is reached, about 10 minutes. Put into warmed jars and seal. Yield: about 3 lbs.

Rhubarb jam

2 *pounds rhubarb, cut small*
½ *pound raw sugar*
juice of 1 lemon
1 *6-inch stalk of angelica, chopped*

Put all the ingredients together in a pan and bring slowly to the boil. Boil rapidly until setting point is reached about 10 minutes. Put into warmed jars and seal. Yield: about 3 lbs.

Rosemary honey

2 *large handfuls of fresh rosemary, about 2 ounces.*
3 *cups water*
1 *pound raw sugar*
1 *tablespoon vinegar*

Lightly wash and chop the rosemary. Put in a pan with water and bring to a boil. Boil gently for half an hour. Strain and add warmed sugar. Stir until the sugar is dissolved, then bring to the boil and add vinegar. Boil slowly until the mixture is of a clear honey consistency, about 30–45 minutes. Bottle and seal. Yield: about 2 cups.

Barberry jelly

Pick the berries on a dry day before they are fully ripe. Strip the fruit from the stalks, and wash. Put into a pan on a low heat and cook gently, crushing the fruit to ensure a good flow of juice. Pour into a jelly bag to drip overnight.

Cook some tart apples in cold water to cover, until they are soft. Leave to drip through a jelly bag overnight.

Allow 1 cup barberry juice to ½ cup apple juice and 1½ cups raw sugar to each ½ cup juice. Bring the combined fruit juices to the boil and add the sugar. Stir until the sugar is dissolved then boil rapidly until setting point is reached, about 10 minutes. Put in jars; leave to cool before covering.

Hawthorn jelly

Pick haws when fully ripe, on a dry day. Remove the stalks and wash. Put them in a pan with 1 cup water to every pound of fruit. Simmer gently until soft, remove from the heat and mash the fruit well. Strain through a jelly bag overnight. To each pound of fruit add 1½ cups of warmed sugar. Bring to the boil and boil rapidly until setting point is reached, about 10–15 minutes. Put in jars and leave to cool before sealing.

Sage jelly

Wash and cut up cooking apples and put in a pan. Cover them with a mixture of water and white distilled vinegar, ½ cup vinegar to every 2 cups water. Add a large bunch of washed and bruised sage leaves. Simmer until very soft. Remove from the heat and strain through a jelly bag overnight. To each 2 cups of juice add 1½ cups of warmed sugar. Stir the sugar until dissolved then boil rapidly for about 10 minutes. Just before setting point is reached add some finely chopped sage leaves. Remove from the heat and allow to cool for a few minutes before potting to ensure even distribution of the sage. Put in jars and leave to cool before sealing.

White currant and elderflower jelly

Put white currants into a pan and cover with water. Simmer gently until soft. Remove from the heat and strain through a jelly bag overnight. To each 1½ cups of juice allow 2 cups of warmed sugar. Dissolve the sugar in the juice and add about 10–12 heads of elderflower—tied together in a cheesecloth bag. Bring to the boil and boil rapidly for 10 minutes, or until setting point is reached. Strain. Put in jars and leave to cool before sealing.

 Chutneys, pickles and relishes

Apple chutney

1 pound apples
1 pound onions
1 pound pitted dates
1 cup brown sugar
1 pound golden raisins
2 cups vinegar
seasoning
cayenne pepper
3 tablespoons fresh chopped applemint
3 tablespoons fresh chopped sweet cicely
a small piece of ginger root

Mince apples, onions, dates and raisins. Add all the remaining ingredients, with the ginger tied in cheesecloth, and stir together well. Cover and leave for 24 hours. Remove the ginger, put the chutney into bottles and cover.

Beet relish

1 pound cooked beets
8 ounces fresh horseradish
½ cup raw sugar
pinch of salt
1 cup white wine vinegar
3 tablespoons fresh chopped dill

Grate the beets and the horseradish. Add all the other ingredients and mix together thoroughly. Put in clean jars. This can be used immediately.

Cucumber chutney

3 pounds cucumbers
2 pounds onion
1½ cups raw sugar
1 cup golden raisins
1 cup crystallized ginger, chopped small
2 tablespoons salt
1 clove garlic, crushed
pinch of cayenne
2 tablespoons dried dill
3½ cups malt vinegar

Peel and slice cucumbers and onions. Put all ingredients into a large saucepan, bring to the boil. Simmer gently until thick, about 1¼ hours. Bottle in airtight jars while hot. This improves with keeping.

Green tomato chutney

2 pounds green tomatoes
1 pound cooking apples
1½ cups raw sugar
2 cups vinegar
1 pound raisins

> 2 *tablespoons fresh chopped chives*
> 3 *tablespoons fresh chopped basil*
> ½ *teaspoon each salt, cayenne, pepper and ginger*
> 1 *clove garlic, chopped small*

Chop the tomatoes and apples and put them into a pan. Add a little water and cook until soft. Dissolve the sugar in half the vinegar. Add it, with all other ingredients, to the apples and tomatoes. Cook slowly until thick, about 45 minutes to 1 hour. There should be no trace of liquid when the chutney is ready. Fill warmed jars and seal. Yield: about 3½ lbs.

Pickled nasturtium seeds

Pick seed pods on a dry day. Shell and place the seeds in a bowl. Cover with a salt solution, made from 3 tablespoons salt dissolved in 4 cups water, for 2 days. Strain. Put the seeds into jars and pour over hot distilled vinegar. Allow to cool before covering. Leave for 6–8 weeks before using.

Tomsitina

> 4 *pounds red tomatoes*
> 1 *ounce mustard seed*
> 1½ *tablespoons allspice*
> ½ *pound shallots, minced*
> 1 *cup raw sugar*
> 3 *tablespoons salt*
> ½ *teaspoon pepper*
> 1½ *cups vinegar*
> 3 *tablespoons fresh chopped basil*
> 3 *tablespoons fresh chopped thyme*

Peel the tomatoes. Tie the mustard seed and allspice in a muslin bag and add to the tomatoes and minced shallots. Boil to reduce to pulp, about ½–¾ hour. Add sugar, salt, pepper, vinegar and the herbs. Continue to simmer until fairly thick. Remove the muslin bag. Put into hot sterilized jars and cover immediately.

Herb vinegars

An easy and pleasant way of preserving your herbs is to make herb vinegars. By a process of infusion with a herb, the vinegar loses its sharp acidity and becomes soft and mellow. Consequently it has a wider variety of uses.

In the kitchen herb vinegars provide useful seasonings in sauces and salad dressings, marinades and mayonnaise, fruit salads and preserves and in many cooked foods.

On the bathroom shelf a herb vinegar made from sage, thyme and savory can be used for bruises and sprains. Rosemary vinegar provides a hair rinse and elderflower or marigold petals provide a facial wash.

Before you begin making your herb vinegars, decide which vinegar you will use. Choose from red or white wine vinegar, malt, distilled or cider vinegar. For a sweet herb vinegar to use in fruit salads, use a cider or distilled vinegar. For a stronger herb root vinegar, such as horseradish or onion, choose a malt or wine vinegar.

When using a combination of herbs be sure that there is not one flavor which will overpower all the others and spoil the blend.

General directions for making a herb vinegar:

1. Fresh leaves are preferable to dried, since they contain a greater amount of the essential oils which provide the flavor.

2. Gather leaves when they are at their best—just before the plants come into flower.

3. Crush or bruise the leaves and fill quart jars three quarters full.

4. Fill the jar with the vinegar of your choice.

5. Cover the jar tightly and stand it in a warm place for 1–2 weeks, shaking the bottle once a day.

6. Taste and, when desired flavor is obtained, strain through a muslin or cheesecloth strainer.

7. Keep tightly corked.

If you prefer to use dried leaves or seeds, heat the vinegar to boiling point and then pour into the jars.

Elderflower vinegar

Heat 2 cups cider vinegar to boiling point. Fill a jar with 1 pound dried elderflowers and pour on the vinegar. Cover and leave for 10 days, shaking the bottle well once a day. Strain and seal.

Add this vinegar to a fruit salad of pears, apples, grapes and bananas.

Garlic vinegar

Crush about 5–6 cloves garlic and place in a jar. Add a pinch of salt. Boil up 2½ cups white wine vinegar and put into jar. Leave for 2 weeks. Strain and seal.

 Other preserves

Gooseberry preserve

1½ cups water
3 tablespoons fresh chopped angelica stalks
2 pounds green gooseberries
2 cups sugar
¼ pound butter
3 eggs

Put the water, angelica and gooseberries in a pan, bring to the boil and simmer to a pulp. Sieve the pulp and place in a pan or bowl over boiling water. Stir in the sugar until dissolved, then add the butter. Beat the eggs until thick and add to the mixture. Stir until it thickens, pour into hot jars and seal. Yield: about 2 lbs.

Honeysuckle conserve

2 cups raw sugar
¼ cup white wine vinegar
½ cup water
1 pound honeysuckle flowers

Choose fully opened flowers. Bring sugar, vinegar and water to the boil. Put in the flowers, bring to boiling point and simmer for 10 minutes. Strain, then re-boil the syrup until thick. Pour into jars and seal at once.

Peppermint flakes

1 cup sugar
⅓ cup water
peppermint leaves

Dissolve the sugar in the water over gentle heat and bring to the boil. Boil until syrupy, then remove from the heat and cover with a damp cloth until cold. Dip peppermint leaves in the syrup until well coated and leave to dry on a wire tray in a warm place. Use in fruit salads and to decorate other foods.

Other strongly scented leaves can be candied in a similar way. For a colorful decoration, dip bunches of cooked barberries in the syrup.

Rosehip syrup

2 pounds rosehips
6 cups boiling water
2 cups raw sugar

Use only ripe rosehips. Chop them coarsely and immediately put them into an enamel pan with the boiling water. Bring back to the boil, simmer gently for 15 minutes. Drain the juice through a muslin cloth. Put the juice into a clean pan and, if there is more than 3 cups, boil it down to that amount.

Add sugar and boil for a further 5 minutes. Pour hot syrup into warmed bottles and seal at once.

N.B. Use small bottles if possible because this syrup has a high content of vitamin C and, once opened, will not keep for longer than 2 weeks.

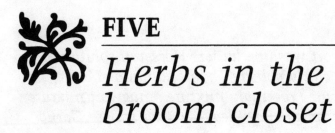

FIVE

Herbs in the broom closet

*Soapwort washing lather • Horsetail solution •
Sweet cicely polish • Thyme solution • Moth
repellents : rosemary mixture : mugwort mixture :
thyme sprigs • Basil leaves • Mint sprigs • Garlic
pot • Lemon thyme sprigs*

Years ago there were many herbs and plants which were used for cleaning, but their preparation and application were time consuming and hard work. There is little advantage nowadays in using them, since efficient ready-made cleaners are so easily obtainable. Nevertheless there are still one or two ways to use herbs for cleaning which are of value today.

Soap substitute

Soapwort washing lather

Put a bunch of soapwort leaves into cold rainwater. Bring this gradually to the boil and boil for 3–4 minutes. Remove from the heat, cover and leave to cool. When quite cold, press through a strainer and pour into a screw-top bottle.

Use rainwater heated to hand hot temperature. Pour into a bowl and add sufficient soapwort concentrate to form a lather.

Use for washing silks, lace and other delicate fabrics. As well as getting them clean, soapwort adds a beautiful sheen and softness to the fabric.

Polishes

Metal polish: Horsetail solution

Make up a strong solution of horsetail, using the fresh herb; for directions see p. 183. After straining, pour the solution into a bowl over the pieces to be cleaned, and leave for 5 minutes. Remove the pieces and allow them to dry thoroughly. Polish with a soft clean cloth or duster.

Alternatively, use a rag dipped in the solution to rub over individual pieces. Again allow to dry and polish.

This is an effective polish for pewter.

Furniture polish: Sweet cicely polish

4 tablespoons white wax (carnauba if possible)
4 tablespoons turpentine
sweet cicely seed

Grate the white wax into a bowl. Add turpentine and leave to melt in the sun or a warm place. Add pounded sweet cicely seeds until sufficient fragrance has been added. Beat until smooth and pour into a wide topped jar and cover. Use on floors and furniture.

Disinfectant

Thyme solution

Make up a double strength solution of thyme, see directions on p. 185, and use it neat for wiping down bathroom and kitchen surfaces.

Pest repellents

Moth repellents

1. Dry leaves of rosemary, sage and mint. Mix together in equal quantities, using roughly a handful of each. Add a

"*A pot of basil set on a windowsill or table will help to reduce the number of flies in a room.*"

little dried grated lemon peel and a pinch of cinnamon. Tie or sew into small muslin bags and lay in drawers or hang in cupboards.

2. For an equally effective mixture, but not so strong, take 3 parts of dried mugwort leaves and flower shoots and add 1 part dried sweet marjoram.

3. Easiest of all, tie long sprigs of thyme together and hang in the clothes cupboard. They will gradually dry while keeping moths away.

Fly repellents

1. *Basil leaves.* A pot of basil set on a windowsill or table will help to reduce the number of flies in a room. Keep it well watered from the bottom so that it will throw out plenty of scent.

Dried, ground leaves left in small bowls or hung in muslin bags in the room are also effective.

2. *Mint sprigs.* Hang up large bunches of fresh mint sprigs to get rid of flies in the kitchen.

Garlic pot for greenfly on houseplants

Put 2 cloves of garlic to grow in a 6-inch pot and place near other house plants. This discourages the attacks of greenfly on the plants.

Lemon thyme sprigs: to repel ants

Cut sprigs of lemon thyme when the smell of lemon is at its highest. Thoroughly bruise the leaves and place the sprigs around the haunts of ants to discourage them.

SIX

Herbs on the bathroom shelf

Angelica syrup • Barberry syrup • Coltsfoot candy • Coltsfoot infusion • Elderflower and peppermint infusion • Honeysuckle syrup • Licorice water • Verbascum infusion • Dandelion infusion • Horseradish embrocation • Horsetail infusion • Marigold leaf infusion • Elderflower ointment • Honeysuckle ointment • Marigold ointment • Marigold petal oil • Mugwort infusion • Marigold lotion • Sage oil • Thyme lotion • Verbascum oil • Basil infusion • Thyme and savory ointment • Mugwort lotion • Herbs for headaches • Herbs for slimming

Herbs were used as remedies long before anyone thought of building a bathroom shelf on which to put them. Herbs and plants constituted the majority of the medicines of old, and using them was the only method then known of healing disease and curing pain. These natural remedies may take effect more slowly because of their mild action, but they will do no harm and should be given a fair trial.

For best results it is important to know how to make the preparations and so use them to the greatest advantage. Unless the remedy is in the form of an ointment, oil or syrup, it will not keep for any length of time. If you need to store infusions, pour them into sterilized jars, or into bottles, and seal. Use them within one or two weeks.

It should be stressed again how essential it is that herbs picked from the wild be correctly identified before being used.

Coughs, colds and sore throats

Angelica syrup

1 cup boiling water
3 ounces (approximately 1 cup) dried angelica stalks
1 cup raw sugar

Pour the boiling water on to the herb. Leave to cool. Strain. Heat the infusion, stir in the sugar and, when dissolved, bring to boil. Simmer until a syrupy consistency is reached. Bottle.

Dose: take a teaspoonful at a time when the cough is troublesome.

Barberry syrup

Follow directions for barberry jelly, p. 163, until all the juice has dripped through the jelly bag.

Put the juice in a pan and stir in 1 cup raw sugar to every 1 cup juice until dissolved. Simmer gently until a syrupy consistency is reached. Bottle and seal.

Dose: take a teaspoonful at a time when the cough is troublesome.

Coltsfoot candy

½ cup dried coltsfoot leaves
1½ cups water
2 cups raw sugar

Crumble the leaves until small. Put the coltsfoot and water in a pan and bring to the boil. Boil for 15 minutes. Strain off the liquid and return it to the pan. Add the sugar and boil together without stirring until a little dropped into cold water forms a hard ball. Remove from the heat, pour into a buttered tin and cut into small sticks when nearly cold.

Dose: suck pieces of candy when the throat is sore.

Coltsfoot infusion
1 quart boiling water.
1 ounce (approximately 1 cup) fresh crushed leaves

Pour the boiling water on to the crushed leaves. Return to the heat and boil gently until the quantity is reduced by half. Bottle and seal.

Dose: take a hot teacupful regularly to relieve colds and catarrh.

Elderflower and peppermint infusion
Pour 3 cups of boiling water over a handful of elderflowers and one of crushed peppermint leaves mixed together. Leave to steep for 30 minutes. Strain and sweeten with honey.

Dose: take last thing at night in bed, when suffering from a feverish cold. To promote perspiration, drink as much as you can as hot as you can. Stay in bed the following day and repeat the dose.

Honeysuckle syrup
Use ½ cup honeysuckle flowers to 1 cup boiling water and follow the directions for angelica syrup on p. 180.

Dose: take a teaspoonful at a time when the cough is troublesome, or for a sore throat.

Licorice water
1 cup licorice roots, dried
1½ cups water

Break licorice root into small pieces. Bring water to the boil and pour over the licorice. Return to the pan and simmer for 20–30 minutes. Bottle and seal.

Dose: sip cold when the cough is troublesome and to ease a chesty cold.

Verbascum infusion

Use dried or fresh flowers; about 7 flowers per teacupful of boiling water. Pour boiling water on to flowers, cover and leave to steep for 6–10 minutes. Strain.

Dose: take 2–3 cups of hot infusion per day for persistent coughs, bronchitis and hoarseness. Take a cupful at night to promote sleep.

Stiff joints and aching limbs

Dandelion infusion

2 *teaspoons fresh chopped root and leaves*
½ *cup water*

Put leaves, root and water in a pan. Bring to the boil. Remove from the heat, cover and steep for 15 minutes. Strain.

Dose: take ½ teacupful hot or cold twice a day for stiff joints and gout.

Horseradish embrocation (liniment)

3 *tablespoons grated horseradish root*
12 *tablespoons pure lard*

Melt the lard in a pan. Add the grated horseradish and stir until it boils. Simmer gently for 20–30 minutes. Press the mixture through cheesecloth or a hair strainer and pour into small pots. Cover when cold.

Use: massage into stiff muscles after a hot bath. Rub gently on to aching and painful joints.

Horsetail infusion

1½ cup dried horsetail
4 cups water

Pour water on to the horsetail and leave to soak for 2 hours or longer. After soaking simmer in the same water for 15 minutes. Remove from the heat and leave to cool. Strain. Bottle and seal.

Use: as a footbath for tired and aching feet. Pour into a bowl and top up with hot water to cover the ankles. Sit on a chair, relax and soak the feet in the infusion for 10 minutes. Dry the feet well and dust with boric acid powder.

Marigold leaf infusion

4 cups boiling water
1 cup fresh chopped young leaves

Pour boiling water on to the leaves. Cover and leave to cool. Strain and use as required or bottle and seal.

Use: as a footbath for tired and aching feet. Follow the directions given for horsetail infusion.

 ## Skin complaints

Elderflower ointment

1 3¾-ounce jar of white vaseline
4 cups crushed elderflowers

Slowly melt the vaseline and add the crushed elderflowers, pushing them down with a wooden spoon. Bring to the boil and simmer gently for 20–25 minutes. Immediately press through cheesecloth or a hair strainer and pour into small pots. Cover when cold.

Use: soothes chapped hands and relieves chilblains.

Honeysuckle ointment

Follow directions as given for elderflower ointment, substituting honeysuckle flowers.

Use: smooth on to skin to relieve sunburn.

Marigold ointment

Follow directions as given for elderflower ointment, substituting crushed marigold petals.

Use: smooth on to the skin to relieve sunburn and for small cuts and abrasions.

Marigold petal oil

2 cups crushed marigold petals
1 cup pure olive oil

Put the herb into a glass screwtop jar and add the oil. Cover and leave in the full sun, either in a greenhouse or on a windowsill, for 4–5 weeks.

After 2 weeks strain the oil through cheesecloth, pressing out every drop. Add a fresh lot of the herb and proceed as before. Shake the jar thoroughly once a day. Finally strain the oil into clean bottles and seal.

Use: dab on spots and pimples and other skin eruptions.

Mugwort infusion

1 cup mugwort flower shoots
2½ cups boiling water

Pour boiling water on to the mugwort and leave to steep for 10 minutes. Strain. Bottle and seal.

Use: an effective remedy for blistered feet. Moisten cotton pads in lotion and gently apply to the blisters. Alternatively soak the feet in the warmed lotion for 10 minutes. Dry the feet well and dust with boric acid powder.

 ## Sprains and bruises

Marigold lotion

Pour 1 cup boiling water over ½ cup marigold petals. Leave to get cold. Strain. Bottle and seal.

Use: dip pieces of cotton balls in the lotion and lay on the sprain. Bandage lightly to keep cotton in position.

Renew the cotton as soon as it becomes dry. Continue the treatment until the swelling goes down.

Sage oil

Follow directions as given for marigold petal oil on p. 184, substituting crushed sage leaves.

Use: rub oil lightly on to bruises.

Thyme lotion

2 cups boiling water
1 cup fresh thyme leaves

Pour boiling water on to the leaves. Cover and leave to steep for 10 minutes. Strain and leave to cool. Pour into bottles and seal.

Use: dip cotton balls into the cold lotion and place on a bruise or sprain. Bandage lightly to keep the cotton in position.

To ease aching limbs, make up a strong infusion and add to the bath water.

Verbascum oil
Follow directions as given for marigold petal oil on p. 184, substituting verbascum flowers. Bottle and seal. *Use:* rub lightly on to bruises. This is also an effective remedy for painful hemorrhoids.

 Travel sickness and nausea

Basil infusion
Pour 2 cups boiling water over 1 cup chopped basil leaves. Cover and leave to steep for 5 minutes. Strain and bottle.

Dose: take a small glassful of the cold infusion just before starting on a journey.

 Bites and stings

Thyme and savory ointment
Follow the directions as given for elderflower ointment on p. 183, substituting half bruised thyme leaves and half savory leaves.

Use: an effective remedy for mosquito bites.
For other insect bites use a poultice of fresh grated horseradish root. Put the horseradish between two pieces of cheesecloth and lay on the bite. Bandage lightly and leave in place until relief is felt.

 Splitting nails

Mugwort lotion
Make up a double strength infusion of mugwort flower shoots, see p. 184. Leave to cool. To 1 cup infusion add 2 tablespoons glycerine.

Use: clean the hands and while wet soak the fingernails in the mugwort lotion for 10–15 minutes. Carry out the treatment once a day. This strengthens the nails and prevents flaking and splitting.

 ## Headaches

To relieve the pain of a headache, drink a hot cup of any one of the following herb teas:

> Elderflower
> Rosemary
> Peppermint
> Sage
> Savory
> Thyme
> Woodruff

Directions for making the teas are on p. 123ff.

A quick remedy for a headache is to press fresh picked peppermint leaves on to the forehead and temples. It is cooling and refreshing.

 ## Herbs for slimming

Some herbs can help the slimmer to lose weight. The retention of fluids in the body is a common cause of overweight. Dandelion, burdock and, to a lesser extent, fennel, lovage and rosehips are all mild diuretics; they stimulate the action of the kidneys, which helps to rid the system of excess fluids.

The herb teas, or infusions, should be taken in conjunction with a calorie-controlled or balanced diet if the weight loss it to be maintained.

Perhaps "on the bathroom shelf" is not the correct place for slimming aids, but an important part of a campaign to lose weight is to take a herb tea first thing in the morning and last thing at night. The basic advice of all slimming diets is just to eat less, and one of the ways in which you will automatically cut down the food intake is to drink a herbal tea about half an hour before each meal. One of the most pleasant teas to drink is *rosehip tea*. Directions are on p. 00, but leave out the sweetening; it does contain some calories. *Dandelion tea,* on p. 123, is a particularly effective eliminating tea. Another way of using it is to express the juice from freshly gathered leaves and roots and take 2–3 tablespoons a day in the morning. Fennel seed tea is a digestive and diuretic; and chewing a few fennel seeds also helps to allay the pangs of hunger. Leaf of sweet cicely is useful to slimmers; used in cooking, it helps to cut down the amount of sugar required for sweetening.

Herbs do not add any calorific value to foods but they do contain nutritious substances which are important in any diet. They can also make uninteresting food much more palatable.

Finally, remember that exercise should play a major role in any slimming program. It helps to burn up the calories and stimulates the eliminating processes.

❦ *Suppliers*

Dried herbs and spices can be found at health food stores and specialty food shops For fresh herb plants, consult the following list. Catalogs are usually available if you send a self-addressed stamped envelope.

Caprilands Herb Farm
Silver Street
Coventry, Connecticut 06238

Casa Yerba
Box 176
Tustin, California 92680

Gilbertie Florists of Westport
7 Sylvan Avenue
Westport, Connecticut 06883

Horticulture House
347 E. 55 Street
New York, New York 10022

Indiana Botanic Gardens
Intersection of U.S. 41 and
Chicago-Detroit Super Highway
Hammond, Indiana 46325

Logee's Greenhouses
Danielson, Connecticut 06239

Nichols Garden Nursery
1190 North Pacific Highway
Albany, Oregon 97321

The Tool Shed Herb Farm
Salem Center
Purdy's Station, New York 10578

In Canada, dried herbs may be obtained from:

The Wide World of Herbs, Ltd.
11 St. Catherine Street East
Montreal, 129, Canada
(Will send catalog free upon request by anyone in US or Canada)

The Herb Grower, a quarterly, is an excellent source of information (Falls Village, Connecticut 06031).

Essential oils

Aphrodisia
28 Carmine Street
New York, New York 10014

Caswell-Massey Co., Ltd.
Catalogue-Order Department
320 West 13th Street
New York, New York 10014

Lanolin, oils, waxes, cocoa butter, fuller's earth, kaolin powder, alum, borax, distilled water, etc.
Most drugstores or order from Caswell-Massey

Caustic Soda or Lye
Hardware stores

Vinegars, vegetables oils, honey, wholegrains, etc.
Health food stores

Index